INVENTORY MANAGEMENT
VOLUME 2

AND SOME OBSERVATIONS ABOUT THE FUTURE
OF THE AUTOMOTIVE AFTERMARKET

PETE KORNAFEL

authorHOUSE

AuthorHouse™
1663 Liberty Drive
Bloomington, IN 47403
www.authorhouse.com
Phone: 833-262-8899

Published by AuthorHouse 09/22/2020

ISBN: 978-1-7283-6968-6 (sc)
ISBN: 978-1-7283-6969-3 (hc)
ISBN: 978-1-7283-7096-5 (e)

Library of Congress Control Number: 2020916087

Print information available on the last page.

This book is printed on acid-free paper.

To Lorraine 1+1 = a million!

"In God we trust. All others must bring data."[1]

---

[1] Most recently attributed to Jeff Bezos of Amazon in Bezonomics by Brian Dumaine, published in 2020. Also attributed to Michael Bloomberg. It appears the quote originally came from W. Edwards Deming.

CONTENTS

INTRODUCTION

This Inventory Management Volume 2 updates some topics in my Inventory Management and Purchasing book published in 2004. The good news is that much of the original book is still "best practice" for forecasting and purchasing inventory for hard goods distributors. However, this Volume 2 book has better ways to address several automotive inventory management issues. So, newer, best practice processes are included here.

This Volume 2 includes new material on SKU forecasting with the addition of external data, a big new section on store assortment planning, some new techniques for managing special cases such as multiple sources, hub-spoke store networks, promotions, category management and supply chain collaboration.

Note that some of these new techniques, particularly assortment planning and promotion management, do not exist in the form described here. They are my own designs with what I feel would be "best practice" for these areas.

And this Volume 2 has some personal observations about the future of the automotive aftermarket in the U.S., with the impact of the Covid-19 pandemic in the (hopefully) short term, and some longer-term factors that will someday profoundly change the aftermarket.

As with my first book, all the examples are from the automotive aftermarket. The owners of the 280 million vehicles in the U.S. all expect that virtually any repair or maintenance job can be performed "today". They expect their vehicle will be fixed correctly the first time and be ready by 5 p.m.

That level of service isn't generally available on many other items. It is unlikely you can get your computer, refrigerator, etc. fixed in one day. That level of service requires a huge investment in inventory very close to automotive service outlets, and managing that is a survival skill for automotive aftermarket companies.

Almost all of the material on purchasing topics in my Volume 1, Chapters 13 to 21, is still appropriate and these topics are not addressed in this Volume 2.

So, if you don't have a copy of my Volume 1, it is available on Amazon, at https://amazon.com/INVENTORY-MANAGEMENT-PURCHASING-TECHNIQUES-AFTERMARKET/dp/1414059086/ref=sr_1_2?dchild=1&keywords=kornafel&qid=1591042994&sr=8-2.

And, thank you for buying this book. As with my Volume 1, all royalties from this book will be donated to the Automotive Scholarship Program within the University of the Aftermarket Foundation. In the 20+ years of the aftermarket scholarship program, more than 5,000 scholarships have been awarded to students planning automotive careers. See the automotive scholarship website at www.automotivescholarships.com.

ACKNOWLEDGEMENTS

I have had the pleasure of working with a number of aftermarket suppliers and distributors on inventory management topics and projects in the past decade, and I have learned much from all of them.

Because of non-disclosure agreements with all of my consulting clients, I can't name names or provide the source of some of the examples in this book, and I can't individually thank each of them here.

I have removed all company identification from examples taken from any of my consulting projects. But, some of my clients might recognize a topic in this book as one that came from their company.

I can thank all of my clients for the opportunity to work with them and their companies on a number of newer inventory management "best practices".

I know I learned more from each of them than they likely learned from me.

I particularly want to thank Schwartz Advisors and all my partners there for providing some consulting projects, a lot of expertise in all facets of the aftermarket, and for permission to reprint some Schwartz Advisor market research.

I thank Bill Hanvey, Auto Care Association, for permission to publish some data from their IHS Markit forecasts and the Auto Care Association Fact Book.

And I'd like to thank Aftermarket Analytics, Babcox Media, Gartner, Harris Williams, Inrix, and the Society of Automotive Engineers for each giving me permission to use their images and data.

Most of all, I thank Lorraine, my wife for 53+ years, and way more than the "better half" of our long partnership.

SKU DEMAND FORECASTING

CHAPTER 1

SKU FORECASTING – LIMITATIONS OF INTERNAL DATA

In the automotive aftermarket, almost all SKUs have a long lifecycle from introduction to obsolescence. This long product lifecycle is the major factor that separates "hard goods" products from "fashion" products.

Fashion Goods – designer apparel, best-seller books, etc., can have very short lifecycles. These are typically just a few weeks or months. The skill and judgment of a merchant and a supply chain that can deliver these items to local stores in a very rapid fashion are the critical factors in accurately forecasting demand for these types of items and delivering superior customer service. Amancio Ortega became one of the richest people in the world by perfecting a very rapid response supply chain over 50+ years at Inditex, principally with the Zara brand and stores.

Hard Goods, at the other extreme, can have lifecycles that last years or decades. Most automotive aftermarket parts fall into this category. One automotive distributor who gave me access to their data has an initial load date of more than 30 years ago on more than 8% of their current stocking SKUs, and that load date is when they first computerized their inventory. Many of those SKUs are even older than that. More than half of those 30+ year old SKUs have sold in the past 12 months at one or more of their locations.

SKU Forecasting Basics:

The demand over the lifecycle of most hard goods resembles a turtle. See Figure 1. The head of the turtle shows there could be some "pipeline" demand when an item is first introduced and some customers add the item to their inventory. Most automotive replacement parts do not begin to sell for actual replacements until the vehicle reaches some initial time or mileage for first replacement. So, there is likely to be a bit of a lull (the neck of the turtle) until these end user purchases commence. Demand should increase over time, reach a fairly stable level for some period, then begin to decline, and eventually die as vehicles that use this SKU are removed from operation and scrapped.

During the periods in the lifecycle when the demand is fairly stable, and when there is a "statistically significant" amount of actual demand data, the internal data is sufficient to forecast demand. If the cycle is stable for a long enough period, that could include SKU level seasonal forecasting, with 2 or 3 full years of demand history.

However, at the transition points, when the lifecycle is in growing or declining demand phases, then point of sale history data is NOT an accurate predictor of future demand. Here is a chart from my first book, with some notes about what data to be used at each stage.

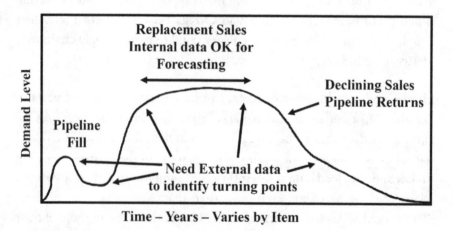

Ch. 1 Fig. 1. SKU Lifecycle Turtle Chart

Forecasting Process with Historical Data:

An ideal system will regularly generate a demand forecast for each SKU at each location in the user's inventory.

The first step in forecasting a SKU can be to analyze existing demand and lost sale history data.

It is important to have "clean" data. An ideal system will be based on actual end user consumption. New merchandise returns should be deducted from net demand in most cases. Shipments to or from customers for "pipeline" activity (adding or removing an item from their inventory) should not be counted. Each user should decide whether to count shipments that are replacements for alleged warranty items.

A good forecasting system will test for SKU level seasonality based on 2 or 3 years of history. If there is a significant difference between the low 2 or 3 months and the peak 2 or 3 months, and if the demand pattern matches closely enough from year to year, then a SKU level seasonal profile can be computed and used. This will let the buyer "look ahead" and compute quantity requirements based on the forecast of upcoming demand.

A good forecasting package will also have a number of features that can help manage the process and alert a buyer when more input or external data is needed. Forecasts based only on historical data can still alert the buyer to any of these conditions:

- The SKU is a new item. It takes at least 6 months of demand history to get anything close to a reasonable forecast. And, that might be biased by the "pipeline" fill – the head of the turtle in the lifecycle chart.
- The SKU has insufficient history for a good statistical forecast based only on historical data. The SKU could be a very slow mover at that location. Several periods of positive demand history per year are typically required.
- The SKU's demand pattern appears to be changing in most recent periods. The forecasting algorithm in my first book included a

"tracking signal". This accumulates signed forecast errors over a number of periods. If the demand is generally level, actual demands over and under the forecast will tend to net out. But, if the item has a significant recent trend, or if it might be at one of the inflection points in the chart above, most of the actual demands will be under or over the forecast, and the tracking signal will grow to a warning level.

- A special process should be used on SKUs before, during, and after a promotion. The demand should be measured against a short term "promotion" forecast.
- The most recent period of demand is way off the forecast. This can trigger a "demand filter" warning. Typically, if the most recent period's demand is ± more than 2 or 3 mean absolute deviations from the forecast, it should trigger a warning. The forecasting package might use the limit value in updating the forecast, or it might leave it unchanged. The recent demand can be an unusual one-time event that shouldn't impact the forecast, or it could be the first period with a new large customer and should count. It is up to the buyer to decide whether to manually reset the forecast.
- Buyers may want to flag some items for manual review, and not use the software at all for those items.

If the SKU passes all these conditions, then a system generated forecast based on historical data should be good for the next demand period, without external data.

But, if any warning is issued, then that SKU forecast should be reviewed.

And external data may help generate a next period forecast.

CHAPTER 2

EXTERNAL DATA IN THE AUTOMOTIVE AFTERMARKET

Best Practice:

For well-established items with sufficient history, local point of sale transaction data can be used to develop a forecast. It can also show, from various warning signals, when external data is needed to develop a better forecast.

There are a variety of types of external data about markets, vehicles, and SKUs that can be used to enhance SKU forecasts based only on demand history.

1. **SKU Application data:** Many "application parts" fit vehicles with very specific year / make / model / engine combinations (YMME). In some cases, it requires "fitment" information as well, to determine the exact vehicles a SKU will fit. There are several catalog data suppliers in the aftermarket who offer YMME to SKU catalog databases, and most aftermarket companies use them for specific SKU lookups, point of sale invoicing, and for purchasing intelligence. For example, Gates K040378 is a replacement serpentine fan belt. Here are a few of more than 80 vehicle year / make / model / engine combinations this belt fits:

Year Range	Make	Model	Engine
2007-2009	CHEVY TRUCK	AVALANCHE	V8-325 5.3L
2007-2010	CHEVY TRUCK	AVALANCHE	V8-364 6.0L
1999-2008	CHEVY TRUCK	SILVERADO 1500 PU	V8-294 4.8L
1999-2008	CHEVY TRUCK	SILVERADO 1500 PU	V8-325 5.3L
1999-2008	CHEVY TRUCK	SILVERADO 1500 PU	V8-364 6.0L
1999-2000	CHEVY TRUCK	SILVERADO 2500 PU	V8-325 5.3L
2006-2008	CHEVY TRUCK	SUBURBAN 1500	V8-325 5.3L
2000-2008	CHEVY TRUCK	SUBURBAN 1500	V8-364 6.0L

2. **Vehicle Registration Data:** Several vendors including Experian, IHS Markit, and Aftermarket Analytics offer databases of vehicle registrations. This is generally referred to as VIO data (Vehicles in Operation). Subscribers can access these databases by the YMME characteristics or other input parameters, and obtain vehicle registration counts by geographic areas, from the full North American market down to individual zip codes in the U.S.

The Great Recession of 2007-2009 had a major impact on U.S. new vehicle sales.

Annual US Light Vehicle Sales

Year	Volume (Millions)
1999	16.9
2000	17.4
2001	17.1
2002	16.8
2003	16.7
2004	16.9
2005	16.9
2006	16.5
2007	16.1
2008	13.2
2009	10.4
2010	11.6
2011	12.8
2012	14.9
2013	15.6
2014	16.9
2015	17.5
2016	17.6
2017	17.2
2018	17.4
2019	17.1
2020	14.5
2021	15.4
2022	16.0
2023	16.3
2024	16.6
2025	17.1

2020 Service Sweet Spot

**Ch 2. Fig. 1. Mind the Gap – U.S.
Light Vehicle Sales History**

As the chart shows, U.S. light vehicle sales were steady at 16-17 million per year from 1999 through 2007. They plunged to 10-11 million per year in 2009-2010. Many feel the best vehicle age range for professional "Do it For Me" (DIFM) repairs is 5-10 years. So, the DIFM segment of the aftermarket experienced a significant headwind from 2014-2020 as there were far fewer vehicles in that prime age bracket. During that same period the "Do it Yourself"

(DIY) segment had a tailwind, as fewer older vehicles were scrapped and more people attempted their own repairs. Starting in 2020, DIFM companies will have a tailwind as the aggregate population of 5-10 year old vehicles increases for several years, and the DIY retail market will have a small headwind for several years with fewer 10+ year old vehicles entering the DIY prime age range of 10+ years old.

Here are just a few examples where the aftermarket is experiencing echoes of the Great Recession.

Ford F-150 pickup sales declined from more than 500,000 units per year in 2005-2006 to less than 250,000 units in 2009, a 50% decrease. They came back strongly, but the big reduction in 2009-2011 models caused a headwind for DIFM the past few years. For perspective, Ford F-series pickup sales reached almost 900,000 in 2019.

The Great Recession did not impact higher income vehicle buyers who buy or lease BMW, Lexus, Mercedes, and other more expensive vehicles as much as it did with businesses and moderate income buyers who buy lots of pickup trucks. While still significant, Mercedes sales declined about 25% during the recession. Other higher end vehicles also had smaller reductions than most of the domestic nameplate lower price cars and light trucks

Of key importance to supply chain managers is the strong year over year changes in VIO for some model vehicles that are emerging into the aftermarket.

One example is BMW 320i. It was reintroduced in 2013 with about 6,000 units sold, and sold about 15,000-20,000 per year in 2014-on. Within the DIFM prime age group of 5-10 year old vehicles, this model went from 5,000 in 2018 (just the 2013s) to more than 50,000 in 2020 (2013-2015 model years). DIFM prime age population will continue to increase for the next few years on this model.

Another example is Buick Encore. It was introduced in 2013 with about 25,000 units sold, but that reached more than 75,000 in 2016. It, too, has a huge jump in vehicle count in the DIFM prime age segment, from 27,000 in 2018 (just the 2013s), to more than 140,000 in 2020 (2013-2015 model years). And this model will have more vehicles in prime DIFM age for next several years.

Companies that supply parts to DIFM outlets should begin stocking SKUs for these BMW and Buick models in many locations, even though they may have little or no demand history for those items.

Be aware of a cautionary note for using vehicle registration data for small geographical areas. A great number of vehicles are not repaired in the local market where they are registered. Many people have their vehicles serviced near where they work, not where they live. Many college students are far away from home, but few get new registrations in their college towns. So, registration data might not be a highly accurate predictor at any specific zip code. But, overall, it can still be a valuable tool to determine the potential market size for many specific SKUs.

Replacement Rate Data: IMR, a major automotive market research company conducts a large survey (about 200,000 households) every year to ask vehicle owners about the maintenance and repairs to their vehicles in the past year. They publish replacement rates for many types of parts and services. Here are some rates from surveys done in past 15 years. These are from the Auto Care Association Annual Fact Books.

As you can see, there are significant decreases in replacement rate for many routine maintenance items – antifreeze, oil changes, filters, spark plugs, tune ups, and more. One unusual cause for this is self-service gas. In the "old" days, all good gas station attendants offered to check under the hood while they were filling your tank. They checked the oil, looked at the battery and cables, belts, washer fluid reservoir, wiper blades, and much more. The last holdout state started allowing self-service gas just a couple of years ago, so no one does these regular quick inspections.

Item	2019	2013	2008	2004	Comments
AC Repair	9%	10%	8%	5%	Now on most vehicles
Air Filter	50%	47%	56%	68%	Less maintenance
Antifreeze Added	27%	27%	22%	38%	Less maintenance
Batteries	29%	31%	25%	24%	More electrical use
Brake Jobs	26%	24%	29%	22%	Pretty steady
Brake Rotors	14%	13%	16%	6%	Now on most vehicles
Brake Shoes, Pads	17%	16%	21%	17%	Pretty steady
Cabin Air Filter	18%	10%	6%	1%	Now on most vehicles
Engine Tune Up	23%	22%	22%	33%	Less maintenance
Exhaust Systems	11%	8%	6%	7%	Not sure why growth
Headlamp Bulbs	14%	11%	7%	4%	Capsules fail faster?
Oil Changed	160%	167%	171%	199%	Less maintenance
Oil Filters	107%	119%	115%	159%	Less maintenance
Scheduled Maint.	46%	43%	42%	NA	Pretty good
Spark Plugs	11%	12%	13%	16%	Less maintenance
State Emission Insp	11%	13%	NA	NA	Not all states
Tires (New)	42%	35%	36%	31%	More miles driven
Wheels Aligned	15%	12%	12%	9%	Goes with more tires
Wheels Balanced	15%	13%	13%	12%	Goes with more tires

Many states have discontinued regular brake and light inspections, but that does not seem to have had a big impact on headlamp bulb and brake replacements.

The "tune up" is almost entirely gone as a routine service. Today, check engine lights and tire pressure warning lights are about all owners have to suggest immediate service needs.

A couple of categories show increases. Battery replacement rates are up, perhaps from the extra loads from many new electrical devices – from seat heaters to onboard entertainment. Tire replacements are up, too, presumably from more miles driven (and perhaps some lower quality replacement tires?)

3. **Replacement Rate Charts:** Large automotive distributors, some distributor groups, and some software companies aggregate point of sale data into large data warehouses. If they use a part catalog database to look up the items for a specific vehicle, some systems can capture the SKU and the vehicle data in their point of sale history. So, they might know, for example, that a Gates K030478 serpentine belt was sold to a specific customer for a 2001 model year Chevy Silverado 1500 with a 4.8L engine.

Combining the SKU application data and the YMME data can give a count of "parts on the road" in a specific market area. For example, a distributor who serves most of one largely rural state has mapped their principal market area. Combining the YMME data with that geographic map reveals there are 69,526 vehicles registered in their market that use the K030478 Gates serpentine belt, and they know the age of all those vehicles. That can be a big help to enhance a forecast based only on historical data.

Combining a very large amount of POS data with the registration YMME data can, with a lot of analysis, generate a forecast replacement rate chart for that type of part. In this example, original equipment quality serpentine belts generally last a very long time, but are typically checked as part of 5 year / 60,000-mile inspections. Some might be replaced earlier as part of a collision repair, or if some mis-adjustment causes premature failure, or if the vehicle reaches that mileage in fewer than 5 years. But, the significant level of replacements will likely begin when the vehicle is about 5 years old. That might be the beginning of the "back" on the "turtle chart" and it might extend for as much as 10-15 more years. As the vehicle age begins to exceed about 15 years or so, vehicle scrappage might begin to diminish the number of vehicles on the road, and start the decline for this SKU.

One company, Aftermarket Analytics, has developed a process to compute lifecycle charts for a number of automotive parts. These show the fraction of vehicles that will need a specific part type by their age. They present these with predictions of replacements by vehicle type – cars, trucks, SUVs and vans.

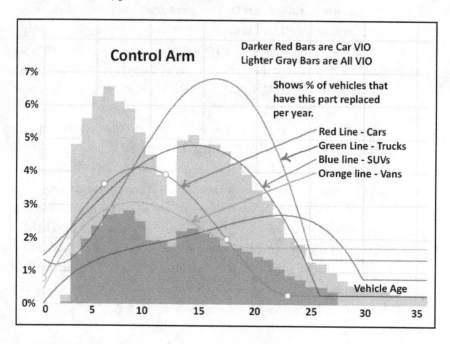

**Ch 2. Fig. 2. Aftermarket Analytics
Lifecyle chart for Control Arm**

With permission from Aftermarket Analytics

For example, this chart shows that about 4% of 10 year old cars will need a replacement control arm. Almost 7% of 16-17 year old trucks will need a control arm.

4. **The matrix:** Combining the appropriate registration data (including the counts by specific model year) with the replacement rate forecast (a table of replacement rate by age of the vehicle) can

produce a matrix of anticipated SKU sales for specific SKU in a specific market area over current and future time spans.

5. **Local Market Sales Data:** One widely used automotive software provider, Epicor, asks all their users to upload their POS data, so they have a very large data warehouse of actual sale and lost sale records, and these may cover a number of competing distributors that operate in any one market. They also have a proprietary application catalog database, and subscribe to VIO data. While they do not let individual users access specific competitors' data, they do offer aggregate analysis to all their subscribing users. And, they have combined all this into an Inventory Optimization Tool. They offer that by subscription as an application called Vista by some distributor groups, Inventory Optimization Tool (IOT), or IPRO by others. The primary aim of Vista is to help with assortment planning, but it can be valuable for existing items as well. There will be an example in the next chapter.

6. **Vendor Data:** Most suppliers issue data on SKUs in their product category. New number announcements (with application information), recalls and obsolescence notices, pricing information, interchanges, images, and more.

   Some suppliers subscribe to the various aftermarket data vendors and have assortment modeling tools to assist their customers in developing a local market forecast.

7. **End User Data:** The very "cleanest" data about actual demand exists at the very end of the entire distribution channel. A part purchased by a retail customer in an auto parts store or a part installed on a vehicle in a repair shop is an actual end user demand. Shipments from supplier to distribution centers and from distribution centers to stores are just "pipeline" movement of goods, and don't reflect any actual consumption. So, if you forecast based on any of those, your forecasts are likely to be

influenced by the "waves" in the channel – goods just moving back and forth.

I always wished I could access and correctly aggregate the actual work order data from our repair shop customers. It would offer a wealth of intelligent detail. It would show parts installed – to be counted as actual demand. It could be used to diagnose parts sold on one job – for a "market basket" approach to make sure we stocked all parts necessary for a job. It could be used to see what parts that shop did NOT buy from our company. That would be a wealth of detail to help diagnose coverage, pricing and more.

Back in the day, one of my favorite shop owners required that I personally call on him every 90 days for a ½ day appointment. He made me go through their shop accounts payable file. He was interested in buying as much as he could from our store, as his shop got better margins on our products than those sourced from car dealers or other parts suppliers. I was interested in that, too. Each visit, I got a valuable list of parts we did not have available in our store, and he got to have very specific discussions with his techs. He would ask his crew what happened when we discovered that our store had a part for a job but their shop purchased it from another supplier. Sometimes it was because the tech wanted the OE part or preferred some other brand. That was an opportunity for us to do some training, and in some cases, to review our selection of suppliers.

8. **Vehicle Dealer Data:** One company, Solera, has collected and aggregated work order data from OE vehicle dealers. This shows specific parts used and the reason for repair – collision damage, scheduled maintenance, or part failure. I believe they still offer subscriptions to this data. It requires a lot of work to translate the OE part to an aftermarket part and then aggregate the data by the type of repair performed. Particularly for aftermarket suppliers, it could be a valuable source of early data on "emerging" parts and

help guide when they should begin to be sourced, stocked, and sold in the aftermarket.

While most items will follow the "turtle" lifecycle chart, there can be differences in the horizontal time scale. Within a single part type, one SKU might begin to fail fairly quickly on some vehicles, while other SKUs might last much longer on other vehicles. So, early replacements can be a leading indicator that a specific SKU is emerging.

9. **Market Share Data:** The supplier trade association, Motor Equipment Manufacturers Association (MEMA) has divisions for Original Equipment Suppliers (OESA) and Aftermarket Suppliers (AASA). The association has several councils by vehicle system – brake, filter, etc. They share but do not publish their member sales data.

   Unfortunately, there is no good 3rd party organization that can help an automotive distributor determine their market share.

   It is likely that a distributor's market share varies widely across the spectrum of SKUs. A distributor who specializes in one or more product categories will likely have a larger market share on those as compared to other lines. There are typically more outlets that carry the top moving SKUs, so it is likely any "full coverage" distributor has less market share on those top moving SKUs, and a higher share of the slower moving SKUs. And, distributors who carry product lines from suppliers to both OE and aftermarket are likely to see much higher market share on SKUs where that supplier is the OE vendor for that vehicle. So, even if you use all the above data sources to generate an independently formed forecast for the demand of a SKU in a specific market, it is still very difficult to convert that to specific SKU forecasts for any one distributor in that market.

ACES and PIES:

Auto Care Association, a trade group of suppliers, distributors, and others, manages an industry effort to provide a database framework for all this data.

ACES, the Aftermarket Catalog Exchange Standard, is a database of vehicle YMME data. This includes a VCdb – Vehicle Configuration database, PCdb – Part Configuration database, Qdb – Qualifier database, and more to provide a complete framework of vehicle configurations.

PIES – the Product Information Exchange Standard, provides a framework for specific SKU information. This include data standards for exchanging product information, attributes, images, hazmat information, interchanges, and links to the VCdb.

These and a number of additional databases are managed by committees within the trade association, and available by subscription to any member users. They provide a complete framework for building, maintaining, distributing, and using vehicle and product data to assist users in determining appropriate SKUs for any vehicle repair or maintenance job.

CHAPTER 3

THE FUTURE OF EXTERNAL DATA

Greatly expanded transmission of vehicle data offers many potential improvements in the future.

Onboard Data: All vehicles manufactured since 1996 have an "OBD Port" – a cable connector under the dash on the driver side. It is a female 16 pin computer cable connector.

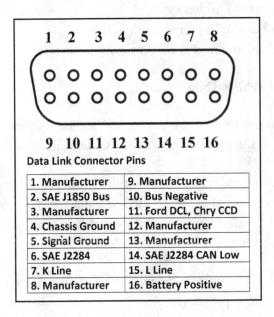

Data Link Connector Pins

1. Manufacturer	9. Manufacturer
2. SAE J1850 Bus	10. Bus Negative
3. Manufacturer	11. Ford DCL, Chry CCD
4. Chassis Ground	12. Manufacturer
5. Signal Ground	13. Manufacturer
6. SAE J2284	14. SAE J2284 CAN Low
7. K Line	15. L Line
8. Manufacturer	16. Battery Positive

Ch 3. Fig. 1. OBD Connector Diagram

A wide variety of diagnostic and other equipment can access the vehicle data by connecting a cable or other device to this port. It is widely used to diagnose fault codes and perform repairs. It is also accessed by state emission inspection stations – to collect stored fault codes and monitor the vehicle during dynamometer emission testing. It can also be used to retrieve all kinds of vehicle data for a number of other uses.

This data is typically stored:

- Real-time parameters: RPM, speed, pedal position, spark advance, airflow rate, coolant temperature, etc.
- Status of "Check Engine" light
- Emission readiness status
- Freeze frame: a "snapshot" of parameters at the time a trouble event has occurred.
- Diagnostic trouble codes (DTCs).
- Oxygen sensor test results
- Vehicle Identification Number (VIN)
- Number of ignition cycles
- Number of miles driven with MIL on
- On 2014 and newer, EDR or event data recorder.

Transmitted Vehicle Data:

The ability to transmit all this stored vehicle data is called Telematics. It is currently used in a wide variety of ways. Here are just a few examples:

1. Over the road trucks can transmit location, speed, engine data and much more. This can be used to build the driver logs, compute miles travelled for state vehicle taxes, help schedule maintenance, and much more.

2. Several insurance companies offer "safe driving discounts" by inserting a proprietary module into the OBD connector that collects and transmits vehicle driving data – speed (vs. local speed limit), miles travelled, hard braking, and more.

3. Some new vehicles have capability for cellular connectivity and local WIFI networks in the vehicle. This is a channel that could possibly transmit vehicle data to other computer systems.

4. Vehicle data can be transmitted to a service provider. This can be used to contact the vehicle owner when a repair or maintenance service is needed and schedule an appointment. The service provider can use this data to preorder parts that might be required for the job. This can expedite the repair and give greater customer satisfaction.

5. Vehicles manufactured since 2014 include an Event Data Recorder. This stores data for the most recent several weeks of use (typically 250 engine start/stop cycles). This can be used as a "black box" for a variety of purposes to diagnose accidents and other driving conditions.

How far can you see?

A personal experience some years ago illustrated some of the benefits that could be gained from full visibility of vehicle data in our supply chain in the automotive aftermarket. I've been thinking about the potential ever since...

I was at one of our auto parts stores, talking with a counter person when he took a phone call. It was from the store's largest customer, a service center just across the street. I listened to one side of the conversation. "Hi Mike" ... "OK, you need a set of front ceramic brake pads for a 2010 Chevrolet Silverado 1500 pickup" ... "Is it a 4x2 or 4x4?" ... Pause, no response. The shop hadn't looked at the vehicle in enough detail. Then, our counter person said "OK, what color is it?" Over time, a few customers have told me what color their car or truck was, but I never thought I needed to ask a customer that question, so I paid closer attention. I heard our counter person say "OK, it is blue" ... Our counter person put down the phone, reached under the counter, retrieved a big set of binoculars and focused on the vehicles parked outside the service center. He soon picked up the phone and said "OK, Mike, I see the blue Chevy pickup, and it is a

4x4. I'll send you the right brake pads." Our counter person said they did that all the time and it was normal, but I was startled and very pleasantly surprised.

Ever since then, I have wished the entire aftermarket had that set of binoculars. Just imagine how much we could improve service to vehicle owners if everyone could see all the vehicles and all the activity in the entire aftermarket supply chain.

It is an impossible goal to give 100% order fill to every customer on every order, with "exactly when needed" delivery, but the aftermarket could come closer to that, and minimize inventory, if it had those binoculars…

Here are just a few examples of what you could see…

On that Chevy pickup, our store sent exactly the right brake pads the first time, because they could see the necessary vehicle specifications. They also saw that vehicle was still parked outside the shop, so they knew they had a little time to deliver that order.

Our store could see that another shop just ordered a brake hose for a vehicle up on a hoist, wheels off, tech standing by, and that the vehicle was promised for 5 p.m. The store would know they had to rush that delivery.

Our store could see that a different shop only used one of the two tie rod ends they'd delivered earlier for another vehicle. They would know the other tie rod end is going to come back as a return. That would let them know they did not have to replenish that item on their daily stock order.

Our store could see their customer shops' estimates for vehicles scheduled for repairs tomorrow and the next day. The store would have time to source some items for those vehicles from their distribution center and still give complete and "when needed" delivery of everything the shop might need for those jobs.

Each of those details seem minor, but scale them across the millions of repair jobs performed every day in the aftermarket, and the potential is astronomical.

Then, extended visibility "downstream" would offer even more potential. We're getting closer to the day when an aftermarket service center would be notified when a customer's vehicle just got a check engine light with a fault code P0132 showing that O_2 sensor #1 in bank 1 is giving no signal. That shop could let the customer know about available appointment times and schedule the work. The serving auto parts store could translate that to an expected order for the proper item, and would know when that part will be needed.

Another vehicle might be approaching 60,000 miles, and the whole supply chain would have time to be ready with items for that maintenance job.

The aftermarket still has lots of work to do to assure access to the full telematics data stream from customers' vehicles, and has to figure out a workable business model for widespread use, but the potential is HUGE.

It would be a gigantic "big data" project, but visibility of all the vehicles near a shop or store, and their mileage, and any OBDII codes, merged with vehicle to part catalog data, could significantly help the aftermarket optimize assortment planning for every store and distribution center.

There would be big advantages to aftermarket distributors with full visibility in the "upstream" direction as well. Almost all auto parts stores can see the inventory at their serving distribution center, but the DCs can't see as much about their suppliers.

Most DCs receive Advance Ship Notices (ASNs) from key suppliers, but few use them to update near future inventory availability and generate emergency orders to maximize their order fill.

A DC could see when all shipments will arrive, match that with their inventory, to schedule receiving work efficiently and prioritize shipments to be put-away first that have the most needed inventory.

A DC could see that a container of imported brake rotors just cleared customs at a U.S. port, and will have much better data about when it will arrive. The DC could plan "fill in" orders properly based on that, to maximize order fill.

A supplier could see all inventory in their entire customer base. It would be another "big data" project, but that could be used to help optimize inventory everywhere in the channel.

A supplier could also see vehicle population and mileage to assist in forecasting and planning for new needed items.

The visibility provided by those binoculars could give a big boost to the entire aftermarket supply chain's ability to fulfill the goal of 100% order fill exactly when needed.

With disparate shop management, store, and distribution center supply chain systems, and incomplete standards for data exchange, it still seems impossible.

But, it ought to be on the industry agenda to work on standards and systems to provide this level of collaboration.

"Your Car, Your Data, Your Choice":

Vehicle manufacturers want to retain all the vehicle data. The aftermarket needs access to it. So, Auto Care Association and the Automotive Aftermarket Suppliers Association – AASA – are jointly sponsoring an initiative entitled "Your Car, Your Data, Your Choice". This is to gain legislation stating that the vehicle owner should be in control of access to the vehicle data.

Auto Care Association has also been working with Society of Automotive Engineers on a "Secure Vehicle Interface" to protect vehicle data from hacking, and control access to it.

Vehicle manufacturers have each adopted unique standards for the data on their vehicles. They know that requiring different equipment to access each vehicle make will create a big challenge in the aftermarket. So Auto Care and the aftermarket are also working with the International Standards Organization (ISO) on a common format for this data.

As more and more vehicles have cellular and wi-fi capabilities, the keys are data ownership and common data formats.

Here is a graphic from Auto Care Association about the "Your Car, Your Data" campaign.

This November, there is a ballot issue in Massachusetts about vehicle owner access and control of their vehicle's data. It could be a landmark event in this fight.

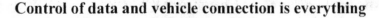

Control of data and vehicle connection is everything

- Your Car/Your Data campaign increasing awareness of the aftermarket's need to be able to directly connect with moving vehicles.
- Secure Vehicle Interface (SVI) concept has had 2 ISO Standards approved (ISO 21177 and 21185) in an 18 month period. ISO 21184 has moved to committee and will be reviewed in 2020

Car Manufacturer's Choice (EVI)   Consumer's Choice (SVI)

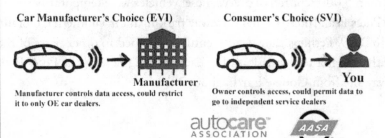

Manufacturer controls data access, could restrict it to only OE car dealers.   Owner controls access, could permit data to go to independent service dealers

Ch 3. Fig. 2. Control of Vehicle Data

With permission from Auto Care Association

Side note on the Volkswagen diesel emission scandal:

In 2014 the California Clean Air Resource Board commissioned studies of Volkswagen diesel vehicles where the US and European versions exhibited different emission performance. Scientists at West Virginia University determined that emission performance varied widely between on the road driving and dynamometer testing – when a cable was connected to the OBD port. They concluded that Volkswagen incorporated software that detected a device in the OBD port. When something was plugged into the OBD port, it caused the engine to operate in a "clean" mode, to pass emission testing. When nothing was in the port, the vehicle software changed to a different mode. That generated much more emissions but got much better fuel mileage.

In 2015, this became a scandal involving more than 10 million VW diesels worldwide and more than 500,000 in the U.S. It became known as Volkswagen Dieselgate. The Chairman of VW resigned, and VW booked a charge of more than $18B for the issue. Volkswagen offered a huge rebate or a new car exchange to affected owners. It was alleged Audi and some other manufacturers might have followed a similar path.

More than 5,000 repurchased VW diesel vehicles were temporarily stored at the Pikes Peak International Raceway parking lot in southern Colorado in 2018-2019. Perhaps they were eventually shipped to other parts of the world that do not test emissions. Fig. 2 below is a photo of the Pikes Peak Raceway site from Google Earth, about 2018.

**Ch 3. Fig. 3. Recalled VW diesels at
Pikes Peak International Raceway.**

Google and the Google logo are registered trademarks
of Google LLC, used with permission.

Additional Volkswagen note:

Shop owners and technicians refer to vehicles with hard to diagnose
problems as "alligator cars". A shop owner told me about one of those
in his shop. It was a Volkswagen diesel and it was getting terrible fuel
mileage. They diagnosed everything they could think of and couldn't find
a problem in any of the vehicle systems or components.

After several hours of fruitless searching, one of the technicians realized
what was causing the problem. The owner had Progressive Insurance,

and had installed Progressive's "Snapshot" device to record driving data. The Snapshot device plugs into the OBD port. That caused the vehicle to assume it was being tested. So, it was running full time in the "clean" mode where it got far worse fuel mileage.

They had to tell that Volkswagen owner he could save money on insurance and spend it on fuel, or vice versa, but not both.

Predictive Analytics and Predictive Failure Analysis:

The vehicle already knows and can transmit odometer readings. So, it is possible for the vehicle to notify the owner and a selected service provider when it is coming up to time for mileage-based maintenance procedures such as 30,000 and 60,000 mile services.

Vehicles can also transmit odometer readings for oil changes based on mileage. Some newer and high-end vehicles can trigger an alert for an oil change based on various measures of the oil viscosity, presence of contaminants, etc.

It is still in the future for automotive vehicles, but lots of work is being done on aircraft and major industrial equipment to diagnose many mechanical and electrical systems and send alerts based on predicting imminent failures. In the not too distant future, your vehicle might be able to tell you and your service provider that it is coming up to time for new brake pads, or that a vibration predicts imminent failure of a bearing or suspension part, and much more.

Combined with Telematics, this can assist service providers in doing all kinds of maintenance and repair jobs.

And, it is just one more step in the data exchange for a service provider to notify their primary supplier that they are likely to need one or more specific SKUs to perform maintenance or repairs on a vehicle that has transmitted any of these conditions.

That will go a LONG way toward making sure the right part gets to the customer just in time for the job.

STORE ASSORTMENT PLANNING

CHAPTER 4

STORE ASSORTMENT PLANNING BASICS

Introduction:

Most of the software available for inventory management is designed to manage a defined inventory. It deals with optimizing safety stock, managing replenishment, and identifying overstock.

But there are few tools available to help define the inventory assortment itself.

There are many factors that enter into inventory assortment planning. Here are a few examples:

- "Art": The skill of a merchant to select items that will sell.
- "Capacity": Can be in many forms. It can be the number of slots in a vending machine, the space available in a category planogram, or the size of a store.
- "Science": For "hard goods", the ability to predict future sales can be used to assort an inventory to maximize income.
- "Goals and Budgets": Setting a service level goal or inventory budget is a critical factor in constraining the planned inventory.

In my experience in the automotive replacement parts industry, defining the inventory assortment for each auto parts store is "THE" inventory management challenge at the store level.

Stock 1 or 0 is the key challenge at Stores:

An auto parts store typically stocks about 20,000-25,000 SKUs from a universe of over 1 million SKU candidates. And, each store stocks "1" (or 1 "per car quantity") of all but about 5,000 of those SKUs.

So, the basic decision to stock any specific SKU, or not stock it, at a specific store, governs about 2/3 of the total store inventory investment in an auto parts store. And, most of the channel inventory is at the stores.

There is some need to forecast the most popular SKUs to set an inventory depth, but most auto parts stores get daily replenishment, so depth on popular SKUs is not as critical as assortment planning at the store level.

Inventory Assortment Basics:

Processes for setting an inventory assortment for each location depend on several key factors. The customer's needs and expectations, the type of product, the lifecycle of the items, the universe of potential items, and history and forecasts for individual SKUs all have a major impact.

Customer Needs and Expectations:

At one extreme, at a custom furniture store, the customer's expectation is that the store will NOT have the item they want in stock. They expect to select the style, fabric, etc. and have the item made to their specifications. Even when the store sells an item, they should NOT use that data to select inventory for stock. It is unlikely that any other customer would buy exactly the same thing again soon.

At the other extreme, at a hospital or on an ambulance, everyone hopes they have exactly what is needed for immediate treatment of any patient crisis.

When I visit an auto parts store, I expect the store to have almost everything in stock for my Ford Expedition. I would be disappointed if they did not have an item for that vehicle. On the other hand, I expect the store might

NOT stock many items specific to my 1967 Mustang, and I would not be disappointed if they had to do a "special order" for an item for that vehicle.

Customer Lead Time Requirement:

The customer's lead time requirement is another critical factor in store assortment planning. For example, here are four categories of lead time requirements that are typical to DIFM professional customers:

1. Parts in 30 minutes or less: A repair shop discovers it needs additional items for a car on a hoist, wheels off, technician standing around, bay tied up, and job promised to be finished and ready by 5 p.m. today. This will require rapid delivery from a brick and mortar auto parts store for as long as the American public expects same day repairs on most vehicles and jobs. A "first call" parts store will continue to "own" this segment of the shop's business for a long time.

2. Parts needed within 2-3 hours: If the shop can schedule the work on a job for later in the day, or if a needed item is not readily available from local stores, then a 2-3 hour lead time window permits shops to broaden their potential sources of supply.

    a. Traditional aftermarket distributors and some majors (especially O'Reilly Auto Parts) can handle orders with this lead time requirement with availability from hub stores or area distribution centers and "loop truck" or other mid-day delivery methods.

    b. Note that Amazon can meet this lead time in the 70+ metro markets where they have a local fulfillment center and offer "same day" delivery (usually by contract drivers). This is Amazon's "Prime Now" service. Amazon has stated they're on their way to 100 fulfillment center DCs. They don't stock many auto parts today, but they will…

3. Parts needed tomorrow: There are lots of professional repair jobs where the lead time for parts can be "tomorrow" and not "must have today". A few examples:

    a. Where the shop expected the repair to take more than a day, and has made an arrangement with the customer for a loaner car or offered a ride to/from the shop.

    b. Where a needed part isn't available locally, and the shop has to hold the vehicle until tomorrow, even if they initially promised the car for today.

    c. Where the shop is willing to order parts today for vehicles with service appointments tomorrow. WORLDPAC trains their customers to do this.

        i. Well organized shops can improve their productivity with this process. For example, suppose a shop has two cars with appointments for tomorrow morning. One has been inspected and is returning for a brake job, and another is a new appointment for a car with the "Check Engine" light on. For the first car, the shop can pre-order brake pads or calipers, rotors, and hardware today and get those parts on their first delivery tomorrow. Tomorrow morning, they can first diagnose the vehicle with the Check Engine light and order parts needed for that job with 2-3 hour delivery. Then, the tech can go right to work on the brake job with all the parts on hand. The brake job can be completed, and then the tech can work on the other vehicle when those parts arrive. The tech and the bay are kept busy, and the shop minimizes the need for "hot shot" deliveries.

4. Parts needed with lead time of 2 or more days: Shops have this lead time on supplies, tools, replenishment orders for shop inventory, and known parts for jobs scheduled 2 or more days from now.

Note that Amazon Prime can provide this service now, virtually everywhere in the U.S., with no additional delivery fee beyond the annual Prime membership.

We don't have data to estimate the mix of a typical repair shop's purchases across these lead time categories. But, a very well-organized shop will have just a small fraction of their overall requirements in the "30 minutes or less" category.

Type of Products and Product Lifecycle:

At one extreme are pure "fashion" items. Next season's designer apparel, best seller books, and other brand-new items have no established demand history, and a "buyer" or "merchant" must use their skill and judgment to establish a forecast. Traditional forecasting tools are no help here.

At the other extreme are established, stable items where demand history can be used to forecast an item's future demand potential. For these items, forecasting software can be used to help define the inventory assortment as well as set basic stock levels and purchasing quantities.

If you work for Zara or Hot Topic, you plan to change a big portion of each store's inventory several times per year. If you work for Tractor Supply, or Ace Hardware, or NAPA Auto Parts, lots of items have been established good sellers for decades, and are likely to continue to be good sellers for the future time horizon you need to plan store inventory assortments.

Most businesses have a mix of these extremes. In our auto parts organization, most of the inventory is in established items where past demand history can be used to provide a meaningful future forecast.

Capturing demand beyond items already stocked:

Stores have a difficult time getting meaningful demand information for items not already in a store inventory. Most store point of sale systems allow employees to enter "lost sale" records, but it takes extra time, and isn't always done. A retail customer walks in, looks around, and walks out empty handed. Perhaps the store lost a potential sale, but most retailers have no practical way of collecting meaningful data on that. A shop uses their shop software to access the store inventory. They discover the item they need is not in stock at the store or available within their lead time requirement, so they order it from another supplier. That is a lost sale, too, but most store computer systems don't retain that "lookup" data. So, some other source of demand data or forecasts is required.

Demand Forecasts: How much data do you need, and what data is appropriate?

A single auto parts store will have frequent sales activity on a few thousand of the most popular SKUs. For those items, a forecast can be derived just from that one store's transactions.

If a single store has a "statistically significant" amount of demand data on a SKU, then the forecast for that SKU in that store could be based strictly on that store's history.

But, thousands of SKUs will have only a few demand "events" in recent history at a single store. In that case, it is necessary to incorporate some more "global" data to develop an accurate forecast.

Store Clusters

A first step beyond the individual store data might be to look at a SKU across a "cluster" of "like stores". This can give more history, and a more accurate aggregate forecast for that group of stores. That forecast can then be proportioned back down to each store based on its contribution to the cluster level forecast.

The challenge is to choose the best configuration of store clusters. You would like them to be as big as possible, as the "law of large numbers" makes those forecasts more likely to be accurate. However, it is just as important to make sure you have "like stores" in the cluster. If you aggregate demand from stores that face dissimilar markets, you average the potential from dissimilar markets, and give a less accurate answer.

In my opinion, it is more important to make sure you have "like stores" in a cluster than to have clusters with a higher count of stores.

"Like Stores"

The market demographics and potential, and the store's configuration and customer base all play into choosing "like stores". One store might be in a relatively high income "do-it-for-me" market. That store should have more potential for premium products, parts for more expensive vehicles, more parts for SUVs and vans, and more "related items" to complete "full repair" and maintenance jobs. Another store might be in a relatively lower income "do-it-yourself" market. It is more likely to sell more "value grade" items, more parts for lower priced vehicles, more parts for pickup trucks, and relatively fewer parts "per job". We have seen a noticeable difference, for example, in items like wheel hub bearings. Stores in "high end" markets are likely to have a bigger mix of sales of the premium grade, and a bigger mix of sales of pairs, as customers choose to replace both wheel bearings even if only one has failed. Stores in "low end" markets are likely to sell a bigger mix of the value grade items, and most sales are for one unit, as customers in these markets are more likely to only do the minimum necessary to get their vehicle back on the road.

In some cases, a single, dominant customer can be the key differentiating factor in determining store clusters. At one time, CARQUEST supplied many of the CarMax used car dealer locations. CarMax was likely to be the largest customer for a CARQUEST store that supplied one of their locations. CarMax sells a fairly uniform mix of fairly new used vehicles in almost all of their locations. And, CarMax performs a standard set of reconditioning services on all their used cars. So, their purchases are fairly uniform across all of their locations. This mix of purchases might outweigh many other market demographics as an influencer of what that store should stock in its inventory. It appeared to be appropriate to cluster "CarMax" supplying stores into "like store" clusters just based on that one factor.

"Big Clusters":

Even with clustering stores, there will still be thousands of SKUs that do not have a statistically significant amount of demand history at the store cluster level to develop an accurate forecast. It is necessary to aggregate an even larger global view, or infer demand forecasts from other data in these cases.

Seasonality and Trends:

Even with good store clusters, it can still be difficult to determine seasonality and longer-term trends just from the aggregated demand history across a relatively small number of stores. In many cases, the distribution center has sufficient data to develop seasonal profiles for SKUs, and those could probably be applied to most of the stores served by that DC.

Qualify Items Eligible to be Stocked at a Location:

It is necessary to qualify items as "eligible" to be stocked at a location. Then, the additional rules can be used to decide whether that is a good investment (or not).

Some items might need to be blocked, and not stocked, even if there is demand for that item at that location. In some cases, there are constraints. Some stores are in locations where local fire codes prevent them from stocking flammable items. Some stores have no loading dock or other way to handle very large items like 55-gallon drums of bulk oil. Some stores do not have space to stock bulky items like exhaust tailpipes, or have an overall size constraint that limits the total inventory size.

This is important for the inventory mix at each store.

It is also a necessary prerequisite to properly post the demand to the correct location, especially in the case of store transfers.

Store Transfers:

It is important to count the demand where you want to stock the inventory, not necessarily where you fulfill the order. This requires some detailed management of the demand accounting.

An example of two extremes... If you are willing to stock an item at a location, then count the demand at that location, even if the product was sourced from another inventory.

If the item is not eligible to be stocked at a location, then count the demand at the location where you want to stock the item.

Store/SKU specific forecast:

The result can be a forecast for every SKU that has had any activity in a store in the past 3 years, and SKUs that are not currently stocked at that store but should be considered. This will typically include forecasts for thousands of items beyond ones currently stocked at that store. Those are all candidates for evaluation.

Assortment "Turnover":

New items are emerging constantly, as vehicles with newly designed parts reach ages where replacements are beginning to occur. Other items are dying constantly as parts that fit only older vehicles decline in sales as the vehicles are scrapped or repairs are avoided.

Approximately 10% of the SKUs in a typical auto parts store will need to be added as new items each year, and a similar number will need to be eliminated from the inventory.

Process:

Traditionally, assortment planning has been a "batch" process, where one product category is reset across all the locations in a company, and typically once a year.

This traditionally has been tied to a calendar – to get a product line ready for an upcoming peak season, or to update all inventories before a scheduled annual stock adjustment return to a vendor.

The next chapter will show one tool to assist in "batch" assortment planning, and the following chapter will discuss a method for "continuous" assortment planning across many product lines.

CHAPTER 5

A BATCH ASSORTMENT PLANNING TOOL

Most distributors traditionally analyze and reset inventories on one product category at a time across all their locations.

EPICOR Vista Example:

Fig.1 is a sample of EPICOR Vista output for Gates Corporation products for a distributor who serves most of one state.

The distributor can set up market areas (by zip code, county, etc.) for each of their locations, and run this for each location. This example is for their full market area.

This report is sorted by EPICOR's estimate of overall product category coverage. In this example, EPICOR estimates the top 22 SKUs (through KO60841) offer 15% coverage of the entire category in the distributor's market area.

The K040378 serpentine belt discussed in Chapter 2 is #1 on this list. The full report has detail with a full list of makes and models each SKU covers.

Part	Stock	Last 12 Mo Sales	Previous 12 Mo Sales	Local VIO	Local Vista Demand	Blended Coverage	Tool Action	Std Part Description	Prominent Make	Prominent Model	Min Model Year	Max Model Year
K040378	Y	213	222	69526	6212.40	1.60	KEEP	SERPENTINE BELT	CHEVY TRUCK	SILVERADO 1500 PU	1985	2010
38001	Y	115	180	460488	4722	2.60	KEEP	IDLER PULLEY	FORD TRUCK	F150 PICKUP	1985	2017
K060923	Y	111	80	63511	4023.20	3.60	KEEP	SERPENTINE BELT	CHEVY TRUCK	SILVERADO 1500 PU	1981	2017
45005	Y	75	135	29123	3892.90	4.60	KEEP	WATER PUMP	CHEVY TRUCK	SILVERADO 1500 PU	1999	2006
K060930	Y	62	78	66462	3423.90	5.50	KEEP	SERPENTINE BELT	CHEVY TRUCK	SILVERADO 1500 PU	1985	2017
43263	Y	95	109	27271	3416.50	6.30	KEEP	WATER PUMP	DODGE TRUCK	RAM 1500 PICKUP	1999	2013
38159	Y	52	63	135954	3176.90	7.10	KEEP	BELT TENSIONER	CHEVY TRUCK	SILVERADO 1500 PU	1999	2009
TCKWP329	N	1	-1	58713	3921.40	7.70	ADD	TIMING BELT KIT	HONDA	ACCORD	2003	2017
43315	Y	53	76	33062	2613	8.40	KEEP	WATER PUMP	CHEVY TRUCK	SILVERADO 1500 PU	1996	2014
38009	Y	64	81	400198	2943.60	9	KEEP	IDLER PULLEY	FORD TRUCK	F150 PICKUP	1987	2017
45006	Y	45	20	22095	2851	9.60	KEEP	WATER PUMP	CHEVY TRUCK	SILVERADO 1500 PU	2004	2009
38006	Y	63	87	372508	2917.60	10.20	KEEP	IDLER PULLEY	FORD TRUCK	F150 PICKUP	1981	2017
33671	N	0	0	233190	3718.60	10.80	ADD	THERMOSTAT SEAL	FORD TRUCK	F150 PICKUP	1991	2017
K060935	Y	63	52	46139	2233.90	11.40	KEEP	SERPENTINE BELT	FORD TRUCK	F150 PICKUP	1979	2016
33661	N	0	0	267564	3635.60	11.90	ADD	THERMOSTAT SEAL	TOYOTA	CAMRY	1988	2017
K060882	Y	38	74	34435	2222.70	12.40	KEEP	SERPENTINE BELT	DODGE TRUCK	RAM 1500 PICKUP	1981	2012
41020	Y	64	76	24026	1805.30	13	KEEP	WATER PUMP	CHEVROLET	IMPALA	1987	2007
38158	Y	30	46	136162	2215.50	13.50	KEEP	BELT TENSIONER	CHEVY TRUCK	SILVERADO 1500 PU	1999	2009
43034	Y	59	75	20411	2208	13.90	KEEP	WATER PUMP	DODGE TRUCK	RAM 1500 PICKUP	1993	2003
41122	Y	43	47	13913	1590.60	14.40	KEEP	WATER PUMP	CHEVY TRUCK	TRAILBLAZER	2002	2012
22554	Y	23	21	80966	1587.90	14.90	KEEP	RADIATOR HOSE	CHEVY TRUCK	SILVERADO 1500 PU	1999	2014
K060841	Y	36	44	17198	1407.30	15.30	KEEP	SERPENTINE BELT	HONDA	ACCORD	2003	2017
33624	N	0	0	134956	2857.90	15.70	ADD	THERMOSTAT GASKET	FORD TRUCK	F150 PICKUP	1962	2016
42097	Y	38	39	15693	1331.70	16.10	KEEP	WATER PUMP	CHEVROLET	IMPALA	1992	2009
TCKWP271B	Y	1	11	32862	3296.60	16.50	KEEP	TIMING BELT KIT	TOYOTA TRUCK	TACOMA PICKUP	1995	2004
K060960	Y	41	43	22562	1559	16.90	KEEP	SERPENTINE BELT	CHEVY TRUCK	SILVERADO 1500 PU	1983	2016
TCKWP298	N	0	-2	34692	2791.30	17.30	ADD	TIMING BELT KIT	TOYOTA TRUCK	4 RUNNER	1998	2010
22437	Y	53	43	83330	1857.70	17.60	KEEP	RADIATOR HOSE	CHEVY TRUCK	SILVERADO 1500 PU	1999	2014
38274	Y	26	43	96894	1615.30	18	KEEP	BELT TENSIONER	FORD TRUCK	F150 PICKUP	2002	2017
43530	Y	30	24	24356	1173.40	18.30	KEEP	WATER PUMP	CHEVROLET	IMPALA	2004	2017
K060905	Y	4	24	14416	1298.50	18.70	KEEP	SERPENTINE BELT	CHEVROLET	IMPALA	1987	2009
K061025	Y	37	40	20338	1542.30	19	KEEP	SERPENTINE BELT	FORD TRUCK	F150 PICKUP	1986	2014

Ch. 5. Fig. 1. EPICOR Vista Example

Reprinted with permission from a consulting client.

Not all vendors and product categories are available (EPICOR charges each vendor to be listed). But it can cover a big portion of a distributor's application product categories.

Distributors can set "weights" on various parameters in the Vista modeling process. They can set a weight factor on the Vista sales ranking (but it is a popularity ranking for the full U.S. market). They can set a weight on the "Local VIO" – the count of vehicles that use the SKU in the defined market (but that does not include any provision for forecast replacement rates), and a weight on Local Vista Demand (the aggregate sales of all EPICOR users who submit POS data to the EPICOR data warehouse. Those weight factors must add to 100%.

Units Per Car:

The Vista model includes maximum "Per Car Quantity" (and that data is also often available from suppliers). For example, most end users buy brake rotors in pairs, even if only one requires replacement. So, most distributors stock rotors in pairs in all locations.

At the other extreme are items like Oxygen Sensors and Multi-Port Fuel Injectors. A vehicle might require up to 4 Oxygen Sensors and one Fuel injector per cylinder. These can be $100-200 SKUs. The majority of sales are for single units, so most distributors do not enforce the Per Car Quantity on these categories. Inventory managers need to make a decision whether to stock the "per car" quantity for each category.

It is suggested that users diagnose their point of sale data to help set up rules for whether to require units per car, or not, on various part types.

A good study for units per car should match up point of sale transactions to one customer over 1-2 billing days. In some cases, a customer wants to buy two hub bearings for one vehicle. The local store might only have one in stock. There might be a second invoice later that day or the next day for the second one, after it is transferred from or sold by a hub store, the distribution center, or some other location.

Some categories show a real mixture of sales in per car quantities and sales in quantities of one. Hub bearings are a big category that likely shows this kind of mixed demand history for most distributors. In one study, there was a significantly higher rate of sales in pairs of hub bearings in the higher quality "first line" and a higher rate of sales in quantity one for the economy value grade. It was concluded that customers willing to pay for the higher quality parts were also more likely to say "fix it right" and replace the bearings on both sides. Customers buying the value grade were more likely to just repair the needed one.

Merchants will still have some tough decisions whether to enforce the per car quantity in categories when sales are really mixed. They might decide to enforce it in larger stores, but not in smaller ones where having one unit in stock might save the sale. The best decisions will come from analysis of a LOT of data.

Advantages of VISTA:

Vista offers a significant amount of "external" data to help a distributor's assortment planning process. The ability to "tune" the model in various ways helps a distributor implement their plan for each product category – with benchmarks for coverage levels, particular part types to be included or excluded, etc.

Additional tools are available to help tailor coverage levels, specify vehicle makes, domestic/import, vehicle age brackets and more.

Vista allows an override to keep an item if local sales were greater than a specified number, regardless of Vista's estimate of the SKU's ranking in the coverage scale. Most stores will keep an item in stock if it has sold 2 or more (or 2 or more per car quantities) in most recent 12 months.

Users who have EPICOR point of sale systems can implement changes suggested by Vista and approved by the user directly to the location's SKU stock levels.

Vista also has some tools to perform "market basket" analysis of related items for one job.

Disadvantages of VISTA:

Vista is a time-consuming process. The output is one product line for one location. You can run multiple locations in one batch, but you get a separate output spreadsheet for each location.

Vista doesn't include SKU cost or selling prices. So, if a financial goal is a constraint, you need to blend the Vista output with your own SKU data to cost the suggested additions and deletions. Unless the user exports the Vista output and merges it with their file that includes pricing, the inventory manager does not know the financial impact of the "ADD" and "REMOVE" recommendations from Vista.

Vista gives no advice on how to set the coverage targets. The inventory manager must pick a target coverage level based on all the elements in the prior chapter about customer needs, expectations, lead time requirement, etc. Then, the user can run the model. Then, the user has to price the suggested changes to see if the result is within the desired budget. It might take several iterations to get a suggested plan that best fits all criteria.

But, overall, VISTA is a LOT better than planning with NO external data.

Please see a more detailed example using Vista data in Chapter 8 on Hub and Spoke Store assortment planning.

CHAPTER 6

CONTINUOUS STORE ASSORTMENT PLANNING PROCESS

This is an overview of a process envisioned to continuously update store inventories by recommending additions of new, emerging items and removal of dying items on a continuous basis across many product categories. The goal is to maintain store specific inventory assortments, tailored by demand forecasts, merchant input, and workload constraints.

The "Batch" way:

As discussed in the previous chapter, most auto parts wholesalers perform annual or semi-annual "stock adjustments" to reset store inventories one category at a time in a batch process. The result is a significant "batch" workload for merchants, store and distribution center teams. There is a long-time span between inventory updates, and some likelihood that inventories are not optimized for local markets. Merchants typically use unit movement forecasts to prioritize items for addition and removal.

The "better" way:

Selecting items for an inventory is investing, so using return on investment tools is a better way to optimize item selection across product categories. Maximizing the forecast profit across the network of stores and products is the goal. This means identifying the best place to invest the next available dollar in inventory, and identifying the least productive inventory items for removal. With that, it is possible to do "continuous store updates" and add and remove a few items from each store every day. On product categories where this is feasible, it can completely replace the product line review/reset process.

The Optimum Solution – a continuous process

In a typical store, several thousand SKUs "die" each year, as vehicles they fit are scrapped, or as people stop making those repairs. An owner of a high mileage 15-year-old car might choose to roll down the window rather than replace a $1,000 AC compressor.

And, thousands of new items are introduced each year, for new model vehicles and for some new categories of product.

The optimum process is one that reacts quickly to emerging and dying items, and drives a continuous process of adding and deleting a few items each day to each location. That flow almost disappears in the overall daily replenishment and return processes, and it almost completely eliminates "stock adjustments" or massive inventory resets that generate big batch product flows.

Inventory Selection is an INVESTMENT Decision:

The optimum solution is to determine the best place across your entire distribution network to invest the next dollar in your inventory – the SKU and location that will generate the highest incremental profit return on its investment. And, equally, to understand the best place to remove the next dollar from inventory – the SKU and store that is forecast to give the lowest profit return on investment.

So, it is appropriate to use projected profit return on investment as the basic decision criteria.

And, if you establish a uniform set of investment rules, and apply them consistently across all locations, you can have a system that will optimize the overall inventory and give every location a "fair" allocation of the available inventory investment dollars.

In the short run, most of a store's operating expenses are fixed, or are not sensitive to minor adjustments in the inventory assortment. Rent, payroll, delivery expense, etc. are not going to vary in the short term if you add or subtract a few items from that store's inventory.

What can vary because of the inventory assortment is sales, gross margin dollars, operating income, and the inventory investment itself.

Stores carry items with a wide spectrum of prices and margins. But, the "event" of making a sale, generating an invoice, handling the goods, and processing the transaction basically generates a "per transaction" operating expense. That is fairly independent of the price of the product sold. It costs roughly the same amount of labor to pick, sell, and deliver a cotter pin as an AC compressor. Optimizing the operating income dollars will help select inventory that delivers the most profitable result for the store.

Continuous Process Overview:

The first step in this process is to develop an Operating Income Return on Investment (OPROI) forecast for every SKU currently stocked at a location, and potential SKUs that could be stocked at that location. The basic data element is a Store.SKU record along with its data. Those Store.SKU records can be ranked by their operating income return on investment. The highest ranked Store.SKU record for an item not currently stocked at a specific location gives the best place in the entire organization to make the next inventory investment. The lowest ranked Store.SKU record for items currently stocked is the best place in the entire organization to remove some inventory investment.

This also gives a total view of how each store inventory is performing now, and with some controls, how much a merchant would add and remove to reset the entire inventory. That is a snapshot of how much would be reset in total.

In my experience, it is not unusual to learn that as much as 1/3 of an automotive aftermarket organization's inventory isn't where it should be. It is also not unusual to discover that some stores need much more inventory adjustment work than others.

Armed with that, merchants can meet with operating people from both stores and distribution centers, outline the work to be done, and set a "pace" for each store. The goal is to identify and approve a planned number (typically about 5-10) of specific new items to be added to each store each day, and a planned number (also typically about 5-10) specific items to be removed from each store each day. The workload must fit within operating constraints.

The Advantages:

Stores like this process. They see new items arriving for their inventory more quickly, and some dusty boxes getting removed from stock. They know they have a better ongoing inventory mix. Properly tuned, stores should see a lift in "from the shelf" service levels. That helps get loyal customers, and somewhat reduces the store workload of sourcing "special order" items from DCs or hub stores. Also, all individual stores feel they have an equal chance at the company's inventory investment dollars.

Distribution Centers like the process. It removes the "batch" work of store update orders and stock adjustment returns. The effort to add a few extra new items to each store each day seems to disappear in the overall workload of store replenishment order processing. And, a few more items each day in returns from each store gives a manageable and level workload in returns processing.

Merchants like the process: There will be a few "hot" new items that should be added to every store on their introduction, but beyond that, this process introduces new items into the pipeline on a gradual basis, and the need for large "stock up" orders is eliminated. The process is even more beneficial on the returns side. Removing dying items gradually, one store at a time, while they are still selling in some other locations and currently active at the DC, allows this dying inventory to potentially be resold by other stores. This can significantly reduce eventual obsolescence or vendor stock adjustment returns.

Management likes the process. They have overall control of the pace of the process, and can set overall control parameters to drive eventual inventory to a target, optimum level. And, this applies a uniform "scoring" system across all product categories, so it assures the next dollar invested in inventory goes to the very best Store.SKU combination. And, the next dollar to be removed from inventory comes from the Store.SKU combination with the lowest profit potential.

Not for every Category:

This process works best for "application" product lines where most SKUs have a "lifecycle". Adding them to store inventories as they begin to emerge and removing them as they begin to die optimizes the overall system inventory.

It isn't needed or workable on many other product categories. "Out Front" products with established planograms are one example. It isn't easy to add another peg hook or shelf slot for an item on a retail display. And, it isn't good to show any empty hooks or shelf slots for items removed. Some product lines might be serviced and possibly managed by other distribution sources, and should be excluded from this process. Some categories (e.g. basic hand tools) evolve so slowly the continuous process isn't needed. Items on promotion should be excluded. In some categories like chemicals the DC requires purchases in cases, and individual containers are not returnable to the DC, even if they are suggested for return by the above process.

Optimum Inventory is a Moving Target:

It must be recognized that new items are announced all the time, emerging items begin to sell in quantities that justify local inventories, and dying items have continuously slowing demand. So, an inherent part of this process is to run the entire model frequently, and use the most current results to select the next items to be added or removed at each location. Each complete run also gives a view of the total inventory status, so a merchant can see whether they are "gaining" or "losing" ground on the gap between current inventories and the current ideal models.

This is an ongoing process. Initial store inventories could be a long way from the forecast optimums based on maximizing gross margin potential using this model. Once the process is started, inventories will begin to evolve. Forecasts (and therefore recommendations) will continue to be updated with periodic results.

So, it is important to measure store inventories versus eventual targets, and store "sales from the shelf" versus an optimum level for each store based on their planned inventory.

A "Stable" State is NOT a static inventory assortment:

In the long run, a "stable" state is one where the acceptable pace of suggested adds and deletes is just enough to "keep up" with the ongoing evolution in item sales potentials in all stores and on all managed categories. Even if a store inventory is perfect today, it will be incorrect by next week…

Merchant and Operating Input, Controls, and Constraints:

Merchant input is critical, for all kinds of priorities and ground rules. Here are some typical merchant inputs. "On shelf availability of brake parts is more important to our customers than on shelf availability of carburetor kits." "We should stock brake rotors in pairs, but we do not want to stock oxygen sensors in full sets." "In a hub store – spoke store group, we want a large inventory of radiators at the hub store, and none at its spoke stores." "Some store inventory items are not returnable at all, or returnable only in the DC minimum selling unit pack size." "At store 123, we have to constrain the inventory to fit the building." "We need to get emerging items into the pipeline more quickly, and purge dying items before they get to zero sales potential." All merchant inputs are incorporated as "weights" to bias the operating income calculation and target inventory plans to fit the merchant's goals. These can be "tuned" on an ongoing basis to achieve the desired inventory mix.

DC and Store Operating management input is also critical, to help establish and maintain a workable and steady pace for continuous additions and returns.

The Economics: An "average" $1.5-$2 million annual sales volume auto parts store might realize as much as $5,000 in annual operating income increases for each 1 percentage point increase in "from the shelf" service level. That counts the full store and DC gross margin on the incremental business, minus some percentage (perhaps 1/3) of those sales that could have been salvaged with a special order (but likely at a higher operating cost and/or lower gross margin).

This model doesn't exist as of now:

Three major, public automotive aftermarket companies have a continuous store assortment planning process in place or under construction.

AutoZone engaged Relex, a company based in Helsinki, Finland, in July, 2019 to provide forecasting and replenishment solutions for their distribution centers, and, I presume, update their assortment planning process.[2]

O'Reilly Auto Parts has had an internal process for continuous store assortment planning in place for several years.

Advance Auto Parts acquired General Parts Inc. and CARQUEST Corporation in 2014. Prior to the acquisition, General Parts worked on a system to frequently evaluate and reset store order points. Some of this model is based on their concept, but this model goes far beyond that, and is based on SKU level operating income forecasts. Advance Auto Parts announced publicly in early 2020 they are beginning to test their own new assortment planning system in their company stores.

---

[2] https://www.relexsolutions.com/news/relex-solutions-to-provide-autozone-with-forecasting-and-replenishment/

A number of software providers, including EPICOR, JDA, and others offer assortment planning modules that include all kinds of additional features. JDA's module includes space planning, planogram generation, and more, for example.

Some software providers use GMROI – Gross Margin Return On Investment – as a way to rank items or categories for assortment planning. As one example, see Palladin Point of Sale Systems.[3] In addition to offering retail point of sale software, they suggest using GMROI to evaluate inventory and various departments within stores.

Bruce Merrifield has long taught distributors to measure customer profitability and use that as a tool to manage pricing and focus on key customers. He offers a nice website with good detail[4]. He is a strong advocate of including operating costs when measuring customer or inventory profitability. In my opinion, forecast operating income is the best measure for store assortment planning, too.

I do NOT have current detailed knowledge of ANY of these assortment planning systems. So, this outline is based on my experience, but it is my own design. I hope you might find value in some or all elements of this proposed model.

OPROI is better than GMROI: Not all auto parts are equal. The store operating costs can vary widely across the spectrum of inventory. It takes the same amount of time to sell, invoice, and replenish inventory for a $200 part as a $2 one. Almost all car wash and wax items are sold to retail customers. Almost all chassis parts are sold to shop customers and incur a delivery cost. If a shop orders 2 brake rotors, a set of brake pads and some brake hardware, that invoice and delivery will include several line items, spreading the cost. One-line invoices and one item deliveries for inexpensive parts are expensive to handle.

---

[3] https://paladinpointofsale.com/
[4] http://merrifieldact2.com/

So, I believe including operating costs for store selling, invoicing, and delivery is the best way to rank items by their contribution to store operating income.

Continuous Process Design:

An external (cloud based) database could be populated with store and DC data and merchant inputs and controls. Store and DC data could be refreshed periodically, and the database could be processed (probably weekly) to recommend detailed changes for merchant approval. The goal is to suggest adjustments to stock levels for specific SKUs in each store. Details of approved changes to Store.SKU stock levels and other data can then be exported to the user's systems for implementation.

The basic data in the database is one record for each Store.SKU combination. The goal is to compute a forecast Operating Profit Return On Investment (OPROI) for each Store.SKU combination, rank those, and then use several qualifying parameters, thresholds, and workload limits to suggest a designated number of items to be added to each specific store inventory, and a designated number of items to be removed from each store inventory.

These will be output as recommended new stock levels for that Store.SKU combination. After approval, a process can be used to update the stock levels and reorder points at each location. Then, the user's normal supply chain systems will add the new items to the store replenishment orders and add the items to be removed to suggested returns to the distribution center.

SKU Profit Forecast: A SKU profit forecast includes the annualized forecast gross margin on each specific Store.SKU combination, less a forecast handling cost to achieve those sales. This starts with an annualized Store.SKU unit demand forecast. That is converted to annualized gross margin dollars using the most specific available price and margin forecasts. An estimated, annualized, "line item operating cost" is deducted from that to achieve an annualized operating profit forecast for each actual and potential Store.SKU combination.

Unit Demand Forecasts: With statistically sufficient data, a reliable unit forecast can be made for each Store.SKU combination. SKU forecasts are likely to be superior and more accurate than product category forecasts, as almost any product category aggregation will mix SKUs at widely varying stages in their life cycle. Additionally, external data can be used to supplement the forecast where there isn't sufficient historical data. See the chapter on external data for more on this topic.

Unit Gross Margin Forecasts: Again, with sufficient data at the specific Store.SKU level, it is possible to produce an accurate gross margin percentage forecast. If there is not sufficient data, it might be possible to combine product category margin goals for sales to wholesale and retail customers with the average wholesale/retail mix for each specific store to do an average gross margin percentage forecast.

Line Item Operating Cost Forecast: It is possible to establish a line item cost to receive an order, pick the item, create an invoice, and for wholesale customers, include some delivery cost. See the discussion below on estimating these costs for each Store.SKU combination.

Investment: The inventory investment required to stock the SKU at a specific location can be determined, and weighted by factors discussed below.

OPROI: The result of that is a forecast for "Operating Profit Return on Investment". The goal of the system is to produce store specific inventory assortments that maximize annualized operating profit return on investment. Selecting items to add to specific stores that have the highest ranked OPROI, and removing items that have the lowest OPROI will achieve that goal.

About the Goal: Customers will have a perception of every store's service level, and it is an important factor in their sourcing decisions.

Many systems classify inventory to try to maximize service levels. The key is the ranking criteria. Ranking items by unit demand forecasts gives too much weight to small, low cost items like fasteners, hose clamps, and hose (sold by foot or inch). Ranking items by dollar demand forecasts gives too much weight to very high price items like fuel injectors, computer modules, etc. In most systems the user sets an arbitrary coverage goal for each category without data on whether that optimizes income.

In my opinion, using OPROI will achieve the maximum operating profit for the stores and still give service levels that achieve customer satisfaction.

Weighting Factors: The "raw data" needs to be weighted by merchant input in each area. These are discussed in detail below:

The model has a number of specific weight factors, to incorporate merchant input and bias the results to improve or reduce the ranking of specific Store.SKU combinations. For all of these weight factors use a default of 1.0. A weight factor higher than 1.0 will bias that Store.SKU combination to get a higher ranking, and rank those items ahead of other candidates. A weight factor of less than 1.0 will result in a lower rank, and reduce the likelihood of adding that item or increase the likelihood of removing it from a store inventory. The end result for each Store.SKU combination is based on the PRODUCT of all these weight factors. Many of these are used to weight the forecast gross margin. Here is a quick summary of all of the gross margin weights:

1. Store Weight: This applies to ALL SKUs currently stocked or being considered for that store. A weight >1.0 might be used for a fairly new store still growing into a large potential market – to give that store a bias for more inventory vs. other stores. A weight <1.0 might be used for a store with limited storage space to maintain an inventory level that is constrained by the size of the building. It is expected this will be used sparingly, only for very unusual stores.

2. Product Category Weight: Applies to all SKUs in that category, in all stores.

    a. A weight >1.0 might be used to increase inventories of "important" categories (brake pads, filters, etc.) The reason for assigning a weight >1.0 is that this one sale results in more than just its pure gross margin. For example, many customers expect every store to have a "full" selection of brake pads and filters. If the store doesn't have an item on the shelf that the customer deems important, the customer might reduce their overall impression of the store, and that might mean smaller total future purchases. Or, if a job requires multiple part types, the lack of immediate availability of one item might lose the entire repair sale. Absent a good way to link specific SKUs with a "market basket" approach or with a "jobs" view, a weight greater than 1.0 might be used on some categories. For example, a merchant might want to give a weight > 1.0 to a category like AC Compressor Fittings. It doesn't take a lot of inventory, and you might lose the sale for a several hundred dollar AC compressor if you don't have the correct relatively low cost fitting to go with it.

b. A weight < 1.0 can be used for categories where immediate availability is not always required (carburetor kits, for example). The customer doesn't expect local availability, and the store is likely to retain the sale even if the item has to be sourced from a hub store or DC.

c. A weight factor of 0.0 will indicate that store doesn't want to stock that category at all. No items in the category will be suggested for additions, and all items in the category that are returnable to the DC will be suggested for return. This can completely block inventory in categories the store doesn't want to stock. For example, stores might accept special orders for some accessories or remanufactured engines, and they would show demand history and a forecast, but they do not want to stock any SKUs in these categories, even ones that might have a forecast that would warrant it.

3. Product Category "Add OK" and "Delete OK" flags. Merchants should be able to set flags to allow or prevent adds or deletes on each specific product category. This could be a way to freeze

inventories where the product category is on a planogram display, or it could be used in other circumstances to block automated transfers.

    a.   Use ADD NO for categories where you do not want the system to automatically add store inventory items. (Or set the category weight to 0.0 to block the entire category).

    b.   Use DELETE NO for categories where you do not want stores to return merchandise on "daily" returns. This might be for batteries, etc. or for lines not sourced from the local distribution center. These will need to be stock adjusted manually, outside this system, but "overstock" could be reported on a Global Overstock Report.

4. Store.Category Exception weights: This weight factor would bias an individual store product category up or down (it could override a "global" product.category weight for this specific store). For example, a store that has several large national account customers who specialize in undercar repairs might want additional bias, just at this one store, for several brake and or chassis parts categories.

5. SKU weights: These will bias individual SKUs up or down at all stores.

    a.   Lifecycle weight. A merchant might want to specify a SKU weight > 1.0 for new or "emerging" parts – to help pull them into more stores sooner as individual stores post initial sales early in the item's lifecycle. A merchant might want to bias very old, dying SKUs with a weight < 1.0 to help pull them out of the pipeline a bit more quickly.

    b.   Popularity Weight. A merchant might want to specify a weight > 1.0 for items that are near the top of popularity rankings on a global basis within their categories. If an item ranks at or near the top in "global" popularity within its product category, the merchant could use this weight >1.0 to make it more likely to recommend adding that item to a store. A weight < 1.0 would discourage stocking items that are slow moving or low rank within their category on a more global basis. These low ranked items might show some "random" sales at individual stores, but the merchants might feel those may not be indicative of any ongoing customer demand for that SKU in that store.

6. Spoke Forecast Weight: If a store has a nearby hub store, then it might be able to rely on the hub for short lead time availability, and that might reduce the need for a "full" inventory at the spoke store. Setting this weight to < 1.0 would somewhat reduce the overall spoke store inventory. Setting this weight > 1.0 is not recommended. Note that this weight should only be applied to SKUs that are stocked at the hub store.

7. Units Per Car Weight Factor: There are two ways to deal with SKUs that have a "per car" quantity, and they work in combination.

   a. The first is a hard flag to "Enforce Units Per Car". If that flag is set to YES, then the algorithm should only recommend items for inventory that "make the cut" based on an investment of a per car quantity, and the algorithm should suggest the per car quantity as the minimum store stock level. Most auto parts stores will want to stock brake rotors in pairs, as they are most frequently sold that way. A store is likely better off with an inventory of 50 pairs of brake rotors than 100 individual SKUs stocked 1 each. On the other hand, items like oxygen sensors are seldom sold in full sets. So, the "Enforce Per Car Quantity" flag should be set to "No" for those kinds of items. There are many categories "in the middle" where sales are made both as "eaches" and in per car sets. For example, hub bearings, ball joints, tie rod ends, etc. In my experience the "high quality" product is more likely to sell in sets, and the value line product is more likely to sell in eaches in these kinds of categories.

    b.   The Per Car Weight Factor serves two purposes.

        i.   For categories where the Per Car Quantity is enforced, it is suggested a weight factor larger than 1.0 be used. On something like brake rotors, this will bias the forecast margin up to help pull pairs into inventory.

        ii.   On categories where the Per Car quantity is NOT enforced, a weight factor slightly larger than 1.0 is still suggested. This is because there are still some instances where the customer wants a set, and might not place the order if only one unit is in store inventory. So, the "second" unit on a SKU is worth a bit more than just its own sale value, as it might make (or break) the sale of a set. This will bias a few of the most popular SKUs into suggesting per car set quantity inventory, and should raise the suggested stock level to the per car quantity on some of these items.

    c.   An analysis of POS history is needed to determine the fraction of sales that are in per car sets for each product category, and merchant input will be needed on the judgment calls for some categories.

Investment Weight Factors: Several weight factors could be used to affect the investment used in the detailed calculations. Here is information on them:

1.   Investment Weight. Most inventory cost is covered by the company's funds. However, there might be some categories with "consigned" inventory or "ledger balance" accounts payable, or very extended payment terms. Merchants might want to reflect this partial outside funding by lowering the company's projected investment in inventories of those items. A weight factor less than 1.0 will reduce the investment in the OPROI computation, and

increase the OPROI. A weight factor of 0.0 should not be used in this case (to avoid any division by zero in the computations), but merchants could specify a low weight value for these categories. That would increase the number of SKUs suggested for inventories in the category.

2.   Core Investment Weight: Most remanufactured SKUs have core deposits. In some categories like brake calipers, the core deposits can be as much or more than the SKU "exchange" cost. On one hand, inventory investments in these items should be based on the "real dollars" of core investment, but the un-weighted OPROI math would give a lower projected return (and recommend fewer SKUs) because of that additional investment. On the other hand, merchants are likely to say customers expect stores to have "full" coverage on calipers, alternators, starters, etc. (but may not expect stores to stock many reman computer modules). So, the merchants could specify a "core investment weight" less than 1.0 in specific categories to reduce the impact of the core value used to compute OPROI. A few vendors subsidize the distributor's core investment. In those situations, a small weight factor or even 0.0 would reduce or ignore the core investment cost.

   a.   An offline study of the legacy inventory data can be used to assess the overall core cost as a percentage of the item cost for categories with SKUs that have core charges, and that input can be used by merchants to set these weight factors to provide some compensation for that additional core investment.

3.   Average Stock Quantity Investment Factor. Most SKUs will be stocked as 1 or 1 per car quantity. A few thousand of the most popular SKUs in typical stores will be stocked in greater quantities, even if the store is replenished daily. These SKUs might have a max inventory of some number of weeks' supply based on their forecast. Some SKUs must be purchased in case quantities, roll lengths for all kinds of hoses, or some other quantity greater than 1. In those

cases, the average inventory will be ½ case, roll, etc. and that should be used to scale the investment.

Operating Cost Weight Factors: Most auto parts are (unfortunately) sold in "eaches". In those cases, the average line item cost times the annualized unit forecast can be an estimate of the Store.SKU operating cost. Some items or categories are typically sold in "per car" or "per job" quantities, and the handling cost for those items can be scaled by an average quantity per sale. It is also possible to forecast an average delivery cost for wholesale customers, and factor that by the typical number of line items delivered on a single order (usually 1.5-2.0 for auto parts), and include some portion of that for items that are sold to commercial customers. This data can be used to develop a factor for an average units per order and an average delivery units per order for each SKU. There could also be individual store adjustments to operating costs for stores with widely different than average payroll scales or rent factors.

Computation Processes:

1. Compute an annualized unit sales forecast for each Store.SKU combination. For freestanding stores, record the forecast in units. For hub-spoke stores, adjust the forecast as follows:

    a. The "hub" store forecast for a Store.SKU combination is the sum of the hub store's forecast based on its own local demands, plus the forecast for that SKU in each spoke store that does NOT currently stock that SKU, since the spoke store will look to the hub store for closest availability.

    b. The "spoke" store unit forecast should be based on that store's local demand, but might be weighted "down" if that specific SKU is stocked at the hub store. In this case, you can reduce the potential for stocking items locally at a spoke store that are available at the hub.

    c. Save these Store.SKU forecasts as first step in computation.

2. Compute the units to be stocked at that store and the units to be used for inventory investment.

   a. The recommended stock level is the LARGEST of 1) 1 unit, 2) the "per car" quantity if the "Enforce Units Per Car" flag is set to Yes for this product category, or 3) the annualized unit forecast scaled by the typical "weeks' supply to stock".

   b. The units to be used in computing the inventory investment is the LARGEST of 1) the stock level from above, or 2) ½ the DC Minimum Selling Units for that SKU. In these cases, the average store inventory investment over time will be ½ case, roll, or minimum DC pack, for chemicals, hose, and other items sold only in packs or rolls by the DC, even if the stock level is 1 unit.

3. Compute the investment required to stock each specific SKU in each store.

   a. Compute the weighted unit cost. This is the unit cost times the Investment Weight plus the core cost times the Core Investment Weight Factor.

   b. Multiply the weighted unit cost times the units to be used for investment to get the dollar investment required to stock that SKU at that store.

$$WtdInvest\$ = StockUnits * (UnitCost * InvWt + CoreCost * CoreWt)$$

4. Compute a gross margin percentage for each Store.SKU combination. This will depend on the amount of store POS history. If there is sufficient history, use the average gross margin percentage based on actual POS transactions for that Store.SKU combination for the past several months. (Sufficient history could be 3 or more fairly recent sale transactions). If insufficient history, use a gross margin percentage from that store's "billing schedule" for that product category, and merchant input for the proper selling level (retail or wholesale) for that product category.

5. Compute the annualized, weighted, gross margin dollar forecast for each Store.SKU combination.

    a. First compute the un-weighted annual gross margin dollars using the annualized forecast units, unit cost, and gross margin percentage from the above.

$$AnnGM\$ = AnnUnits * UnitCost * [\frac{1}{(1 - GM\%)} - 1]$$

    b. Weight the gross margin dollars by the PRODUCT of all weighting factors, including:

        i. Store Weight (an overall weight for all SKUs in that store).

        ii. Spoke Store Forecast Weight (Note that this only affects SKUs stocked at the serving Hub store).

        iii. Product Category Weight: (a weight for all SKUs in that product category).

        iv. Any Store.Category Exception Weight. (Use this value to override the general Product Category weight for this specific store.

        v. Two SKU Weights: The Lifecycle Weight and Popularity Weight.

$$WtdGM\$ = AnnGM\$ * StoreWt * SpokeWt * ProductWt \\ * LifecycleWt * PopWt$$

6. Compute the annualized Operating Cost for each Store.SKU combination:

$$OperatingCost\$ \\ = AnnUnitDemand * StoreCostWeight \\ * \left(\frac{OrderCost}{\frac{Units}{Order}} + \frac{DeliveryCost}{\frac{Lines}{Delivery}} \right)$$

a. It is necessary to assign a variable cost per "order" (invoice) and per "delivery".

b. The database design could have average units per order estimated for each SKU.

c. The database design could have a factor for the percentage of a category sold to a wholesale customer (likely delivered) vs. DIY customer (no delivery cost).

d. The database design could have a store level operating cost weight factor to scale these based on individual store operating cost history, to compensate for "high rent" vs. "low rent" and/or "high payroll" vs. "low payroll" cost locations.

e. These are used to weight the operating costs.

7. Compute the annualized Operating Profit for each combination:

$$OperatingProfit\$ = WtdGM\$ - OperatingCost\$$$

8. Compute the OPROI for each Store.SKU combination. This is the annualized operating profit forecast dollars divided by the weighted investment based on the computed number of units to be stocked.

$$OPROI = \frac{OperatingProfit\$}{WtdInvest\$}$$

9. In cases where the SKU has a "per car quantity" that is not "enforced, and where the recommended stock level is less than the per car quantity, two OPROI records should be created. One is for stocking the suggested quantity (without considering the "per car" weight factor on gross margin), and one for stocking the "per car" quantity, including the "per car" weight on gross margin. Evaluate both records against the rest of the "add" opportunities.

10. Compute New Suggested Stock Levels: As part of the overall process, the database could compute a new suggested stock level

for each Store.SKU combination (see step 2.a. above). Those should be compared to the current, existing stock levels for that Store.SKU combination. If the model suggests a higher stock level, the increment should be considered as a potential ADD to the store inventory. A simple model would use the new computed OPROI for this Store.SKU combination in the ranking for potential ADDs. A more complex model would compute a marginal OPROI based on the incremental forecast margin and incremental investment to increase the stock level for this Store.SKU combination. If the model suggests a lower stock level, the excess quantity should be considered for DELETE from that store. In these cases, use zero OPROI for the excess quantity – since it is "overstock" – and flow that into the overall ranked list for potential recommendation for DELETE. Either way, Store.SKU combinations with suggested changes in stock level should make the overall ranking for further consideration for ADD or DELETE selection.

11. Rank that entire list of Store.SKU combinations from highest to lowest OPROI.

12. Select Store.SKU rows of data that meet the various qualifications and restrictions for ADDs to store inventories.

    a. OPROI exceeds "ADD" Threshold. There should be a minimum OPROI threshold for "ADD" candidates. Only Store.SKU combinations with a forecast OPROI above the ADD threshold will be considered. Disqualify all candidates with a lower forecast OPROI.

    b. DC Stock Flag "OK". There should be an "OK" or "NOT" stock flag in the DC database. It is suggested that only items already stocked at the serving DC should be suggested for addition to any of the stores in that market. You might disqualify candidates where the DC does not stock that SKU.

    c. "OK for ADD" flag set to OK.

d. Verify that the item is not already stocked at the store, or that the computed quantity to stock is greater than the current stock level at the store. If the item is already stocked, use the OPROI for the incremental inventory quantity.

e. Select the appropriate number of the highest ranked candidates for each specific store. There could be an ADD items per day value for each store. Start by selecting that number of items times the number of days between processing runs. For example, if this is run weekly, and "Days to Process" is 5 (for 5 weekdays per week), then select 5 x the number of add items per day for that store. Some users might want only 4 days of activity – to not process adds and deletes on busy Mondays. Adjust the number of items per day per store to get the overall weekly pace you want. There could be a MAX Adds per day for each DC. There could be a mismatch between the sum of the individual store "add" number and the aggregate DC number for all stores it serves. See the note below on pacing the overall process and rationing the workload.

f. Within equal ranked items based on OPROI, rank items with the highest gross margin dollar value for addition first.

g. Output those records as suggested ADDS to an Output Data Table, for merchant review, updates and approval.

13. Select Store.SKU rows of data that meet the qualifications and restrictions for DELETE from store inventories.

a. The candidate list includes all items now in stock at the selected store.

b. Weighted OPROI below the DELETE Threshold. There should be a global maximum OPROI threshold for DELETES. Only Store.SKU combinations with OPROI forecasts below the threshold should be considered for DELETE.

c. DC Return eligibility "OK". There will be SKUs that are ineligible for return from stores. Or, SKUs that are OK to return to the DC but only in the DC selling increment pack size. (For example, if the DC sells some chemicals only in cases, it may disallow returns from stores of "eaches" on that SKU.) Only items that meet the DC qualification for return should be considered.

    i. There should be a separate query report to show store inventory in SKUs that are "overstock" according to the database model, but are ineligible for return to the DC. This could be presented to merchants periodically for review and a separate process to purge this undesired inventory.

d. "OK for Delete" flag set to OK for this specific Category.

e. If the user stores a flag for "New" items for a period of time, block store deletes of those items while that "New" code is still in effect. This will prevent returning "New" items before real demand begins to emerge.

f. Don't delete items with good recent sales. The user can select a number of actual store unit sales as an override to DELETES. If this Store.SKU history shows actual sales equal or greater than that number in a defined period, do not delete the SKU from this store. This could hold a SKU in a store even if the weighted OPROI suggests deletion. It is suggested 2 or more per car quantity sales in past 12 months be used to hold an item in the store, regardless of the weighted forecast OPROI.

g. Maintain a "stock until" date at the Store.SKU level. To avoid churning, a time span should hold an added item in a store for some length of time – to a "stock until" date.

h. Also evaluate reducing the stock quantity from the current level to a lower level that still has a sufficient OPROI to retain some inventory at the store. It should be OK to reduce the stock level for this Store.SKU combination during the protected time period, just don't take it to zero.

i. Select the appropriate number of the lowest ranked candidates for each specific store. Use a DELETE items per day value for each store. Start by selecting that number of items. There is also a MAX DELETEs per day for each DC. There could be a mismatch between the sum of the individual store "delete" number and the aggregate DC number for all stores it serves. See the note below on pacing the overall process and rationing the workload.

j. Within equal ranked items based on OPROI, rank items with the highest dollar investment for delete first.

k. Output those records as suggested DELETES to an Output Data Table, for merchant review and approval.

14. It will be necessary to offer a view of each detailed computation, showing all the factors used and the result. This will help merchants diagnose the result, and view all the factors used in each result. That is necessary to help merchants understand the detailed computations, and maintain/adjust all the weight factors and exceptions.

Global Report "Dashboard": The database could generate a global overview, with "drill down" capability, to show the overall status of existing inventories, forecast sales and gross margins, suggested additions, suggested deletions, merchandise in store inventories ineligible for return to DCs, and in categories where the Add OK and/or Delete OK flags are set to block the automated processes. See Fig. 1 as a sample "screen shot" for a dashboard design. This will let an inventory placement manager view status, progress, and workload for any choice of products and locations.

This could allow the user to select all stores and lines or drill down on either or both. It shows the past and forecast inventory levels, store "sales from the shelf" service levels, and the pace of add and delete SKUs per day. Versions of this could be stored to measure ongoing progress. This could become the main "management" report to gauge overall status and progress.

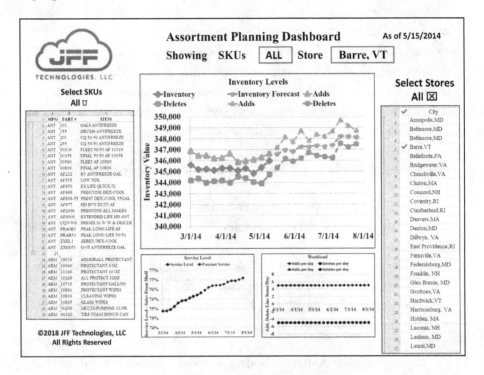

Ch 6. Fig 1. Store Assortment Planning Dashboard Design Concept.

Inventory Recommended Change Output: The Output Data has this period's recommended ADDs and DELETEs that meet all the above requirements. This could be a web interfaced report, with "drill down" capability by DCs, stores, and product categories, to individual Store.SKU combinations. There could be a "high value" flag to highlight individual Store.SKU data rows that involve an investment higher than some control value for additional merchant review.

    a.   The merchant should have the capability to add rows, adjust quantities or "stock until" dates, or delete rows from this suggested output.

    b.   Merchant "approval" should be recorded.

The approved data could be output in a format that the store operations person could use to update Store.SKU stock levels in each store's inventory database. It will likely take an intermediate step to parse the overall batch of approved adds and returns into a daily batch of update records for each store and DC system. That would also allow varying the workload by day of the week. Then, the regular store operating systems should take care of executing adds and deletes as part of the normal store replenishment ordering and store return processes. The "stock until" dates should be migrated back into the database for future processing runs.

Design for Multiple Users/Roles within one or more companies:

All of the above is based on a single company system where any authorized users have access to all data in all tables.

A full "cloud" solution might include degrees and levels of access in the user registration – which tables, which records within tables, and "view" or "add/delete/update" capability. Here are three levels of complexity that could be included in an overall system design.

1. The simplest design is one database where any authorized user has access to view and update any/all data tables.

2. The second level is for larger companies where they may want to restrict users to just their area of authority.

    a. For example, a company might have multiple merchants who each manage a portion of the product categories, and they may want those merchants to only have access to update their assigned records in appropriate product categories.
    b. And/or, they may be organized by locations – and want specific users to only have access to data on specific stores and DCs.
    c. Ditto for the output tables. They may want the output segmented by locations so multiple inventory placement managers would only view/update their assigned portion

of the file, and output files can be coordinated back to the user's operating systems.

3. The third level is a design that would permit multiple companies to use this – with completely separate data in all tables. An economical solution for this might be multiple instances of the overall database.

Notes for possible system enhancements:

1. Note on pacing the system and prioritizing ADDs and DELETEs within workload thresholds. If the sum of the ADD items per day for each store is less than the DC Max Adds per day, no rationing is required on additions, and the DC can handle the max additions to each store each day. If the sum of the stores adds exceeds the DC limit, some rationing is required. It is suggested that merchants adjust thresholds or workload limits to balance the system within operational capabilities. Ditto on deletes. For example, a merchant may want to adjust the max number of additions per day in specific stores that are better or worse than overall average conditions.

2. Note on processing frequency: Most companies use monthly demand history keeping periods, and update forecasts monthly. Even in that environment, it is suggested this process be run weekly to look regularly at "fresh" data.

3. Note on mechanisms to avoid "ping pong" merchandise transfers. It is likely that "one more sale" of some SKU at some store will be enough to lift that item up to an "ADD" recommendation if it is not already stocked at that store. It is also likely that the following one or more periods might not show another sale for that item, and a refreshed forecast might be lower, and drop the item back to the "DELETE" range. There are two mechanisms to control the pace of store inventory adjustments.

   a. The "Zone of indifference". A single value of OPROI as the "cut line" for both ADD and Deletes could lead to this "ping pong" as Store.SKU forecasts are refreshed each period. To avoid that, there should be some gap between the minimum "ADD" OPROI threshold and the maximum "DELETE" OPROI threshold. For example, a merchant might select 0.75 (75%) as the OPROI for the minimum ADD threshold, and 0.25 (25%) as the maximum DELETE threshold. Store.SKU combinations with OPROI values in that gap will be left alone. Initially, it is expected there will be a great many suggested additions, and a fairly high threshold could be used. And, initially, it is expected there will be a great many suggested deletes, so a fairly low threshold (even zero or a negative value) might be used. As the process refines and improves store assortments, these values could be adjusted by the merchant to a narrower gap, but some gap is recommended on an ongoing basis.

b. The "Stock Until" date. Once a merchant accepts a recommended Store.SKU combination for ADD, that item ought to stay in that store for at least a defined period of time, even if no further sales reduce the OPROI forecast below the DELETE threshold. It is suggested that something on the order of 12-15 months be the minimum time to keep a newly added item in a store. The database might suggest a reduced stock level based on updated forecasts, but should not suggest removing the item completely from inventory.

4. Special Product Categories: Some categories may have defined planograms for displays. Merchants may not want to allow deletes and show empty shelves or hooks to customers, and may not want to allow "adds" because of the difficulty of realigning the shelves or displays for single item additions. These categories can be excluded from the process and maintained manually, or the "no delete" and "no add" flag can be set, and/or "protect until" dates could be loaded against all SKUs to prevent deletes before a defined batch stock adjustment date.

5. Note on Hub-Spoke Store groups. See the separate chapter on Hub and Spoke store planning.

6. Note on SKU Popularity and Lifecycle Weights. Here are some suggestions on establishing these weights on individual SKUs.

   c. Popularity Weight. It is suggested to use a ranking of global popularity within each product category and a sliding scale of popularity weight from something greater than 1.0 for the highest ranked item in the category to something less than 1.0 for the lowest ranked item.

   d. Lifecycle Weight. Absent accurate "lifecycle" information on most SKUs, this can be estimated by using a year over year trend in global sales for SKUs in each category. SKUs with year over year increases could be assumed to be "emerging" items, and SKUs with year over year decreases could be assumed to be dying. Here again a weight of something greater than 1.0 for SKUs with largest year over year growth declining to a value less than 1.0 for SKUs with largest year over year decreases. External data such as VIO counts could be used to increase the weight on emerging items and decrease the weight on dying items.

   e. And, there could be some interplay between these two SKU weights. Here are two examples:

      i. "Prevent Early Death". Users may want to block any downtrend on relatively new items or items with significant, even if declining global unit sales. We don't want to "discourage" continuing to stock items that are new, or items that are still globally popular, even when they might show a bit of a decline in demand.

      ii. Find "Emerging Items" earlier: Users may want to block any negative Popularity weight for SKUs that are reasonably "new" and/or have a strong uptrend. This speeds up the response on emerging items, even if they're still pretty far down on the ranked sales within their category.

f. Note on "Replaced Parts". The general mechanism for superseded items is to "sell out" the old item and start replenishing it with the new item location by location as the old item is sold out. It is up to the user's systems to mirror this with the SKU forecasts. Here is a suggested process

    i. Continue to order (and sell) the old item at all locations. DC orders for the old item will help the vendor exhaust their pipeline inventory.

    ii. When the vendor starts substituting the new item on DC shipments, set the old item order flag to zero at the DC, load the new item, and add the old item demand history to the new item's history array. This should set a forecast for the new item to keep going with replenishment inventories.

    iii. Do that same process between the DC and its stores. Stores should continue to sell and reorder the old item, to purge the DC inventory. When the DC starts substituting the new item to a specific store, load the new item in that store, and move the stock level and store history to that new item. That one store will start reordering the new item. Do this on a store by store basis, to help sell out the pipeline of old items.

    iv. At some point, while there are still some sales for the old item at the DC, but sufficient DC inventory of the new item, recall the remaining old items from some stores and replace them with the new item. If you do this in several partial steps across all stores, you can purge the pipeline of the old item without interrupting availability of one or the other at all locations.

7. Note on "Sell out but do not reorder". It is suggested that one of the user's Store.SKU status flags be "Sell out but do not reorder". If that flag exists in the user's systems, it could be the first step toward winding down pipeline inventories on items that are beginning to decline in demand. Individual stores would sell any existing inventory, but NOT reorder it, even if they have a stock level. Eventually, their forecast is likely to decline enough that THIS system would update the stock level to zero for that Store.SKU combination. Otherwise, stores will continue to replenish items up to the day some system decides they should be returned.

8. Note on "per car" quantities in categories where the "per car" quantity is not enforced. The model suggests evaluating both stocking the suggested quantity (usually 1 unit) and the per car quantity.

    g. For "adds" consider both the incremental investment opportunity to add the SKU or to increase the stock level on the SKU to the per car quantity from its existing stock level, using the "per car weight factor" on the margin calculations done for the per car stock level. An example might be in hub bearings. The decision might be whether to add a 2nd unit of a SKU where the store already stocks 1, to get that SKU up to the per car quantity, versus adding 1 unit of a SKU not already stocked.

    h. For "deletes" on SKUs already stocked in categories where the per car quantity is not enforced, the reverse situation exists. A declining SKU might reach the point where it makes sense to reduce the stock level from the per car quantity to a lower number, but leave some units in stock. Evaluate that as well as completely removing the SKU from inventory.

9. Note on dual lines and quality grade coverage. Most stores stock more than one quality grade in many product categories, and have application parts in more than one brand in some categories.

For example, most stores carry "good", "better", "best" lines of brake pads, and most stores carry some coverage in several brands of popular categories like filters. If it is possible to aggregate the history and forecasts for SKUs that fit the same application, that could greatly enhance this model. There will be instances where it is better to add one SKU of a brake pad that gives the store coverage for a new vehicle versus adding a different SKU that gives the store stock in a second quality grade on an existing vehicle.

    i.   If this is possible, it is recommended that the evaluation be done for items not currently stocked at all based on the forecast for the "application" (front disc brake pad set for 2010 Ford F-150) using aggregated forecasts for all SKUs that fit that application.

    j.   Then, an additional set of merchant rules could be used to decide which specific quality grade or brand to stock first.

    k.   Overlapping coverage in other quality grades or brands should be evaluated on just the demand forecast for those SKUs.

    l.   The rationale here is that the store is likely to make a sale if it has some coverage for the application, even if that might not be the buyer's first choice. "You asked for Bosch spark plugs for this vehicle. I've got Champion brand plugs in stock and can deliver them now, or I can source the Bosch plugs and deliver them some time from now." The store is still likely to make that sale (and should log a "lost sale" for the Bosch SKU).

10. Note on customer / brand "loyalty" versus "substitutability". It is important for merchants to understand customers' loyalty to specific brands. Loyalty tends to be higher for the premium grade products. If loyalty is strong, then stores must stock that brand or lose sales. If customers will accept substitutions, then merchants and stores have more flexibility to aggregate demand for specific applications, and stock a suitable brand. For example, some customers specifically want K&N, Bosch, etc. when shopping for

a premium filter, but that same customer might accept the store's private label when shopping for a filter in the economy grade.

11. Note on appropriate level of demand aggregation: The "global" demand for a SKU would be a good guideline on how to aggregate forecasts for that SKU. For example, SKUs that are in the top 10% or so of total company sales should be considered for stocking in every store. Slowest moving SKUs should be stocked only in individual stores that show sufficient demand to merit inventory.

12. Note on "Lost Sales". It is a judgment call to log a "lost sale" for a SKU. There can be many reasons for lost sales, with "price" and "availability" (within the needed lead time) at the top of the list. Most auto parts businesses have relied on store personnel to do this, so training is key. If a customer asks for availability and price of an item, and then doesn't order it, the store person has to judge the reason. Some store POS systems can include a "reason" with a lost sale event. In general, if the item is in stock and the customer still doesn't order it, then price or other brand preference might be the cause. If the item isn't in stock then it might be a lost sale that should be logged to demand.

    a. WORLDPAC has automated this in their B2B Speed Dial system. Since customers look up just one part type at a time in Speed Dial, they know the customer is inquiring about a "front brake rotor" or "front brake pad set" and not just "front brakes". If the customer's store has the item in stock and the customer doesn't order it, they feel price or brand preference must be the issue. But, if the store doesn't have the item in stock, they log a partial lost sale against that Store.SKU combination just from the B2B inquiry. This has been a powerful tool to help them find emerging items to stock.

13. Note on "Self-Fulfilling Prophecies". It is much more likely that the store will get the sale when the item is in stock. A store might only

capture a small percentage of the sales if the item has to be sourced and that adds to the lead time. So, inventory classification can become a "Self-Fulfilling Prophecy". Here is an old-time example:

    a. A merchant decides an emerging item is now "good enough" and begins to stock it in many stores. Future sales are much higher just because the item is in stock in most stores, so the merchant will look at those results and say "I was right".

    b. A merchant decides a declining item is no longer "good enough", and removes it from many store inventories. Future sales decline a lot because the item is no longer in stock, and the merchant looks at those results and says "I was right about that one, too".

    c. The only way to combat this is with some form of external data that helps justify the stock/no stock decision.

14. Note on "related items" and "Market Basket". It would be extremely helpful to have data on items that are frequently sold together. Few systems have the capability to link multiple SKUs sold on one order, to help assure stores stock all the items for a job. For example, it would be very helpful to have links to "left and right" struts, calipers, control arms, etc. While those kinds of relationships are generally specific to make/model/year combinations, other linkages are much more difficult to determine just from catalog database information. A muffler might go with a number of different tailpipes, depending on the vehicle. An ideal system would analyze POS invoices (or, even better, shop repair orders) to find related item linkages. This would be very helpful, but it is far beyond the capability of most IT systems today.

SPECIAL PURCHASING SITUATIONS

CHAPTER 7

MULTI-SOURCE PURCHASING

There are several situations which can result in a single SKU being available from multiple sources at different costs and lead times.

- In many retail categories, some SKUs are available from "expeditors" as well as from their regular source.
- In the automotive parts aftermarket, many SKUs that are sourced from offshore manufacturers are available two ways – from a supplier's domestic distribution point, or direct from the offshore supplier's factory.

An automotive aftermarket example is brake drums and rotors. Virtually all of the U.S. foundries closed years ago, as the costs of complying with EPA and OSHA rules became unaffordable. As a result, almost all of today's brake rotors are imported. Value grade and OE equivalent quality grade products are available from a number of suppliers in China, and from some suppliers in Canada and Mexico. OE equivalent and premium grade rotors are available from some European suppliers such as Brembo from Italy. This discussion will use a typical Chinese supplier as the example.

The Chinese supplier probably has a U.S. domestic distribution center. SKUs are available from that distribution center at a quoted price, and typically with about 10 days lead time from placing an order to product on the purchaser's dock.

That same supplier typically offers direct import programs. These require full TEU (Twenty-foot Equivalent Unit) container orders, and typically require full or half pallet quantities of each SKU. The lead time is usually 60-70 days total, from placing an order to product on the purchaser's dock. However, these orders carry special pricing, which can be 16-20% below the U.S. source of supply cost.

Regardless of how the aftermarket distributor sets their resale pricing, all of the direct import buying advantage, plus or minus any additional inventory carrying and handling costs, accrues to the distributor's income.

Brake drums and rotors are a huge category for the automotive aftermarket. A large aftermarket distribution center might sell enough rotors to efficiently purchase several containers per week. So, it is a category well worth the effort of optimizing the purchasing process.

Most larger distributors use both sources of supply. Faster moving items can be purchased in direct import containers in pallet or half pallet quantities. Slower moving items and any needed "fill in" quantities of fast movers can be typically purchased in "each" quantities from the domestic location, with higher cost, but much shorter lead time. For some SKUs, there can be open purchase orders from both domestic and import source locations.

First, evaluate the economics and set the strategy. Next, evaluate what is needed in the user's supply chain software system to correctly handle both kinds of purchase orders.

Economics:

There are three factors to consider.

1. Acquisition cost differences: The product of the quantity ordered times the cost advantage for direct container orders vs. domestic "fill in" orders.

2. Handling cost differences: If the distributor has "pallet pick" locations for direct import SKUs, there can be an additional

savings in handling costs in the receiving process. A full pallet can be easily checked in, and moved with a fork lift to a pallet pick location. On fill-in receipts, each unit must be scanned or inspected to check it in, and individually handled to move it from the dock to a stock shelf location.

3. Carrying cost differences:

$$Annual\ Carrying\ Cost = \frac{Avg.\ QuantityOrdered * Unit\ cost * Carrying\ Cost\ Rate}{2}$$

Consider an item where a distribution center sells 1,200 units/year with a regular cost of $30. These can be ordered on "fill in" orders in any quantity, or on pallets of 100 units with a special cost of $25.20 (16% discount). Assume it costs $10 to handle each "fill in" receipt, and $10 to handle a full pallet receipt. Assume a (big) 40% annual carrying cost rate.

With Fill in orders: The classic EOQ order quantity for "fill in" orders is about 45 units, or an order about every two weeks. Annual handling cost = $260 (for 26 orders/year @ $10/order). Annual Carrying cost = $270/year (45 units * $30 unit cost * 40% carrying cost rate / 2). Total cost = $530/year.

With Pallet direct orders: Purchase cost savings = 1,200 * $30 * .16 = $5,760. Handling cost = $120 (12 pallets per year X $10). Carrying cost = $504 (100 units * $25.20 * 40% / 2). Total cost = MINUS $5,136/year.

Net savings on this one SKU are just over $5,500 per year on about $30,000 of annual purchases. Virtually all of the purchase price savings flow to income, as the handling cost savings almost cover higher carrying cost for larger "cycle stock" with pallet purchases.

It is clearly better to order this item in pallet quantities once a month to achieve the lowest total cost.

Here is a chart of the Economic Order Quantity Analysis (EOQ) costs with the various costs for this sample SKU. It clearly pays to order this SKU in pallets.

A real-world consideration not included in the above math is "forecast accuracy". If your forecast is way off, you might inadvertently order a lifetime supply of some item. In the real world, even with this level of savings, it likely doesn't make sense to order more than 3-4 month's supply of any one SKU at one time.

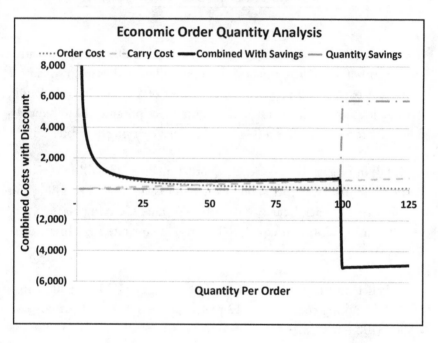

**Ch 7. Fig 1. Order Quantity Analysis
for Sample Brake Rotor**

Supply Chain Software:

Auto parts distributors typically place fill-in orders for major product lines at least once a week. If a SKU has also been ordered on one or more full containers, an ideal system would not show the "on order" quantity for those direct import orders until they are almost due to be received, so the regular replenishment software could still evaluate the need for an interim fill in order. Most of today's software systems do not correctly handle this, and that makes it difficult to see if short lead time fill-in orders are needed even for SKUs generally purchased on direct import container orders.

Best practice would be to have a system that can track (and update) the expected arrival date for each outstanding purchase order. Then the replenishment system could properly consider "on order" quantities that are expected to arrive within the "order up to" number of days from now, and use that to compute an available quantity. The available quantity would be units on hand plus expected units on order minus any units owed to customers on backorders. That could be compared to the "order up to" level to see if an order is needed now.

And, the system should compute both a "fill in" suggested order and a "direct container" suggested order (with both using the correct number of units expected to arrive during those two time windows.

The system should also project the service level over the two upcoming time periods. If the service goal can be maintained over the correct upcoming time span, then no order of any size is required today. If the projected service level will fall below the goal in the shorter time span, then a fill in order should be done today. If the shorter-term service level is projected OK, then a container order should be done today.

Without the correct approach, two significant errors are possible, and both hurt service levels and overall profits.

- The system might keep recommending "fill in orders" and the company would lose out on the potential extra operating income from the direct orders, or,
- The system might keep recommending container orders, and short-term service levels (and corresponding operating income) could also suffer.

Impact on Lead Time Forecasting:

Most distributors that use both types of orders experience significantly different lead time and lead time variability results. Most "fill in" orders typically arrive within a day or two of the projected time, so the lead time forecast can be very accurate and lead time variability can be small for the fill in shipments. On the other hand, lead time can vary widely on container direct shipments. One recurring issue is the impact of the Chinese New Year holiday on imports from China. Most Chinese factories shut down for at least two weeks for this holiday, and it can also impact transportation and container loading within China as well. Even excluding this holiday, lead times can vary by 2-3 weeks for direct import container orders, with hard to predict times spent waiting for ships, customs, ports, and transportation both in the source country and here. That additional lead time variability requires some extra safety stock on container orders.

Even many advanced supply chain systems still have just one lead time forecast and one measure of lead time variability for each SKU. Ideally, a system could maintain two separate forecasts of lead time and lead time variability for each type of order, and use that to compute suggested order up to levels including seasonally adjusted usage over the projected lead time and safety stock quantities based on the lead time variability for each type of order.

Opportunities for automotive (and other) hard goods distributors:

In addition to brake drums and rotors, automotive distributors have access to offshore suppliers in a number of other categories. Full container "deals" are available on CV axles, radiators, filters, and some other product categories. Even with domestic suppliers, distributors have both "fill in" and full truckload pricing with discounts on oil, anti-freeze, freon, and some other high-volume products.

And, some third-party logistics providers offer the opportunity of assembling full containers of products from multiple suppliers. This service can be obtained from providers at a number of Asian ports, and could allow a distributor to obtain savings on multiple smaller product categories where full containers of one product are not efficient.

CHAPTER 8

HUB AND SPOKE STORE ASSORTMENT PLANNING

Many types of distribution companies operate a variety of location sizes, and use broader inventories in larger locations as a nearby and short lead time source of supply to smaller locations.

This has a formal structure as a network of "hub store" and "spoke stores" in some companies.

For example, in the aftermarket auto parts industry, here is some public data on O'Reilly Auto Parts (Stock symbol ORLY) based on their 12/31/2019 annual 10-K report filed at the SEC.

As of 12/31/2019, O'Reilly operated 28 regional distribution centers. These DC locations average 400,000 square feet and stock an average of 159,000 SKUs. They provide overnight delivery to all store locations.

O'Reilly operated a total of 5,439 store locations in the domestic U.S. on 12/31/2019. The typical store is 7,400 square feet and stocks 22,000 SKUs.

In addition, O'Reilly operated 356 hub and super hub stores at 12/31/2019. Hub stores have an average of 42,000 SKUs and super hub stores have an average of 68,000 SKUs. These support the local "spoke" stores typically with several mid-day deliveries and roughly 1-2-hour lead time.

The full spectrum of automotive aftermarket parts is huge – many millions of potential SKUs. Even with a specific selection of vendors, most aftermarket distributors have more than 1 million SKUs in their master inventory data base files. And, like some other categories, auto parts have a very "long tail" with a small number of very fast-moving items and a huge number of very slow-moving items.

A typical local auto parts store can give only about 75% "sales from the shelf" coverage of the full spectrum of demand with its 20-25,000 SKU inventory. A "hub store" can give about 85% coverage from the 45-50,000 SKU inventory. A distribution center can give 95% -97% coverage from 150,000 – 175,000 SKUs. All aftermarket distribution companies rely on prompt and often overnight shipments from vendors to fulfill the remaining 3-5% of end user demand.

And, it is still almost unique that vehicle owners expect most automotive repairs to be completed in one day.

So, the automotive aftermarket really relies on same-day logistics for the vast majority of its sales. That makes tens of thousands of local stores, thousands of hub stores, and at least daily replenishment of those locations from distribution centers an integral part of the distribution channel for the automotive aftermarket.

A couple of automotive examples might help illustrate this:

In general, the goal is to maximize fulfillment of the customer's needs and expectations.

Brake parts are typically the largest product category for auto parts stores. The repair shop needs prompt delivery as they've almost always promised the vehicle will be ready for pickup same day by 5 p.m. And, the shop expects their local auto parts store to have a broad inventory because this is such a major category. Hub stores can help supplement demand for slow moving SKUs, but having a wide inventory selection at local stores is first priority in this category.

In the "middle" size categories by sales volume, replacement radiators present a special case to automotive distributors. There are several thousand potential SKUs, and the best sellers are still very slow-moving items. They are large and fragile. They require a lot of store space and unique racking for good, safe storage. This is a category where the repair shop typically needs 2-3-hour lead time. Even after a repair is diagnosed, it might take the shop that amount of time to remove the existing unit and be ready to install a replacement. At one typical aftermarket distribution company, the top 20 radiator SKUs (typically what a small store might carry in inventory) account for only about 15% of the total dollar demand in the category. It takes about 75 SKUs to cover 50% of total demand. So, the customer likely expects the local store might not have a particular SKU in inventory, but will still order it if it can be delivered in 2-3 hours. With that, some distributors who have hub-spoke networks have elected to stock no radiators at the spoke store locations, and support all spoke locations with a larger inventory at the hub stores. It is still necessary to rely on the distribution center for slower moving availability, and many units may still not be available "same day".

Radiators are such a broad category that it is difficult for many traditional full line auto parts companies to give great local, prompt availability. As a result, it is one category where online vendors who offered very full coverage made good penetration of the market. One of the early companies, 1-800 Radiator made large inroads versus traditional "brick and mortar" distributors. It was successful enough to begin to begin to franchise local specialty distributors as well, and currently has about 200 local specialty stores. Some of those also carry other product categories that fit the same profile with many slow moving, expensive SKUs and parts where a shop can typically wait 2-3 hours for delivery. For example, the local 1-800 Radiator franchisee in Denver carries radiators and AC compressors (another category with many slow moving, expensive parts, and where the shop typically will allow 2-3 hours for delivery).

At the other extreme, small product categories like carburetor repair kits present a much different situation. Most repair shop customers expect the local stores will NOT have the SKU in inventory. And, most customers likely have a different need. It is likely the vehicle is NOT promised for 5 p.m. today, so the shop has one or more days to obtain the item. In this extreme category, it may be possible to operate successfully with no inventory at the local or hub stores, and rely on the DC and vendor for all sourcing.

General Principles for hub-spoke networks:

The process of assortment planning must take a joint view of local and hub store inventories.

- At the hub store: The demand forecast for a SKU at a hub store should be forecast based on the sum of 1) the local demand history for that SKU, PLUS 2) the demand history for that SKU at every spoke store that does NOT stock that SKU, and 3) any external data for that item. That is because each spoke store that doesn't stock the SKU will look first to the hub store for prompt availability of that item.
- At the spoke stores: The demand forecast at a spoke store should be based only on its local demand history plus any external data. If the item is available from a nearby hub store, and if it is a type of item where the customer will typically accept 2-3 hour lead time, then it is somewhat less important to stock it at that local spoke store, as the customer will still order it, even if it is not in the local store inventory.
- So, the network of hub and spoke stores should be jointly planned. In practice, this may require an iterative process, to evaluate SKUs at spoke stores, then plan hub stores based on that, and iterate until a best joint solution is determined.
- For emerging items, it may make sense to add them to a hub store first, and the above process will do that. When no stores stock the item, the hub forecast will be based on the aggregate demand of the hub and all its spoke stores. So, the hub store is likely to be the first location with enough demand and lost sale data to stock the item. Spoke stores will add the item only when their local demand merits it.
- For dying items, the above process may help manage the inventory, too. An item is likely to reach the point where it should be removed

from inventory at one or more of the spoke stores first. When that is done, the remaining spoke demand forecasts will be aggregated into the hub store forecast, so it is likely the item will be retained at the hub. Removing items from one location at a time helps manage the overall inventory and reduce eventual obsolescence or need for returns to vendors.

- A complete hub-spoke store assortment planning process should include additional controls for product categories. As in the above example, it may be desirable to stock no radiators at any spoke stores and focus the full category investment in a larger inventory at a hub store. This might apply to AC compressors, Engine Control Computer Modules, etc.

- Controls might also be required at the SKU level. As one example, some stores might not have the special equipment to handle 55-gallon drums of lubricants, remanufactured engines, or other very large items. They typically require special 2-wheelers and a delivery truck with a liftgate. And, the customer will usually accept 2-3-hour lead time for many of these. These and similar SKUs might be blocked at some spoke stores and carried only at hubs as well.

Hub-Spoke Example using EPICOR Vista:

Here is an example of one product line for a distributor that has their DC and two branch locations in one city. They shuttle parts between the locations all day, so any customer can get a part from any of the locations in a satisfactory time.

The distributor had a "full" inventory in each of the three locations. But, with the shuttle capability, it only makes sense to stock a specific SKU at one of the branches if that branch has sufficient "local" demand for that SKU.

So, in this case, the suggested best practice really increased the suggested inventory at the DC, and really reduced the inventory at the branches.

That allowed a significant increase in overall coverage (to 95% of EPICOR Vista's total coverage in this category).

It also required moving a lot of inventory between the locations, and will require returning or selling down a lot of what was duplicated inventory across the 3 locations.

Control	Value				Chassis and Control Arms
Vista Coverage Level for ADD	95				Add SKUs to get this target Coverage level
Max Model Year for STK N	2004				Discontinue SKU if newest application older than this
Sale + Lost Sale Control Qty	2				Add if demand + lost sale = or > the control quantity
Recent Date Limit	1/1/18				since the control date
Suggested ADD	At Hub	Branch 1	Branch 2	Total	
Total SKUs	892	1	-	893	ADD If Vista coverage under ADD target, OR SKU has
Total $ DC Cost	32,075	44	-	32,119	sufficient sales + lost sales in time period AND fits vehicle newer than control max model year.
Suggested Reductions					Remove if coverage is beyond ADD level and SKU has
Total SKUs	449	295	221	965	fewer than control quantity of sales + lost sales since
Total $ DC Cost	14,199	8,264	6,482	28,945	control date.
Current Inventory At Cost	73,476	10,173	8,855	92,504	So overall is about $3,000 increase. Big increase at Hub
Inventory after actions	91,352	1,953	2,373	95,678	and big reductions at spoke locations.

Ch 8. Fig. 1. VISTA Hub-Spoke Example

Reprinted with permission from a consulting client.

CHAPTER 9

INVENTORY INFORMATION VISIBILITY

For Commercial Customers:

Inventory visibility at the end user customer is critical to providing good service. The customer needs to determine the exact part, and then see availability. If the item isn't available from the end user's regular store, they need to look "upstream" and see both availability and lead time for delivery. Most professional repair shops have one "first call" supplier, but also have access to several other local stores. Quality and availability rank at the top of most professional customers' priorities, and pricing typically ranks below that. A good point of sale system can provide all that data to the end user customer.

One distributor, WORLDPAC, integrates information about the delivery time with their availability information. Their system knows the local delivery schedule to each customer. It also knows the delivery time details for shipment from all their other locations, and the "deal" with that specific customer for who pays any package delivery fees. So, their online system gives these kinds of messages:

- The item is available from your local store. Order this item in next 12 minutes to make your 11:30 a.m. scheduled delivery.
- The item is not available from your local store, but...

- o The item is available at another store in the area. Order it now and it will be delivered on your 1:30 p.m. scheduled delivery.
- o Order this item with additional freight cost for delivery tomorrow by 8:30 a.m. (This would be shipped priority overnight from a master distribution center.)
- o Order this item for no-charge delivery tomorrow by 10:30 a.m. (This would be shipped standard overnight from a regional distribution center.)

- This level of visibility gives the customer control and they can select the delivery choice that best meets their need.

Marketing data including features and benefits of specific products is critical, too. A shop might be preparing an estimate for a brake job. Their system is online with their "first call" supplier, and they can see the cost and availability of a variety of items. A great presentation of lots of data would let them see several items in varying price and quality grades. For example, they might be able to say to the vehicle owner "We can do the full brake job for $199 with original equipment quality parts, or, for $30 more we could use the ceramic brake pads that offer increased braking performance, no brake dust on your wheels, and a lifetime guarantee. You could do that for increased peace of mind and security for your family…"

For Online Customers:

Many distributors perform "fulfillment" services for various online auto parts websites such as Rock Auto, Amazon, eBay, and more.

A number of companies offer data "integration" services. They offer data such as basic information about the part, catalog information to allow a look up from the vehicle information, "fitment" notes, images, product features and benefits, and more. These can be combined with the seller's inventory information to let a retail online customer determine the correct part, select from various brands and quality grades, and order it online, either for pickup at a local store or for shipment to home.

Alternate items – and "overlapping" coverage across brands and quality grades:

It is important to offer information to the customer about multiple vendor and or quality options. At my company, our past "home grown" system had several types of linkages on SKUs that fit a single application. We showed the customer all options and some remarks to help guide their selection:

- "When gone use…" This was used for superseded items. Our system would continue to offer the original item as long as we had inventory in the system. However, demand for that item would accrue to the newer, superseding item. The principle was to exhaust our inventory of the original item, and build up inventory in the new, replacement item. Absent the link, all of the original items are likely to be overstock and become obsolete.
- "Can use…" This was used where we had duplicate coverage of a part for a specific item from multiple vendors. We planned to stock both, and let the customer make his selection based on his preferences.
- "Prefer to use…" This was also where we had duplicate coverage but felt one item was superior to another. This type of alternate record also had a message field with the reason for our preference – better quality, lower price, etc.
- "Can use, BUT…" This was used where we had duplicate coverage but not quite identical items. Here again there was a message field so the end user could see our comments. These could be things like unit of measure differences (some items were boxed each and others in "per car" sets). Or, it could be a case of one item that could be replaced by two others (a welded exhaust assembly that could be replaced by a muffler and tail pipe. Or, any other required explanation about differences important to the end user.

In all cases, presenting the user with full information, images, installation tips, related items, etc. will maximize sales and customer satisfaction, and minimize product returns.

CHAPTER 10

PROMOTION MANAGEMENT

Promotions are one of the more difficult projects for any purchasing and inventory management team, and typically one where most software systems have few tools to help manage the full process. This is somewhat redundant with Chapter 11 in my original book on Inventory Management and Purchasing. Please refer to it for the basics, and here are some additional considerations.

In general:

Selecting the items to be promoted and promotional pricing is usually the responsibility of the merchant for that category. In many cases, this is a plan to pass through promotional pricing and terms from one or more vendors. In some cases, a promotion can be developed around a seasonal theme. An automotive example might be "Get your vehicle ready for winter" – with promotional pricing on batteries, wiper blades, windshield washer solvent, lighting, winter tires, and more. If this is an annual promotion, prior years' results can be used as a guideline for planning.

In other cases, the goal might be just to make sure the entire distribution channel is ready for a peak season. It is very normal to promote air conditioning parts, freon, and related tools and equipment each spring, to make sure that wholesale customer shops are ready for the summer AC business.

So, here are some suggested steps to follow:

Initial Planning:

- Select items, set pricing special pricing, and promotional dates. See the chapter end note on a suggested profitability analysis for promotions.
- It is important to identify the promotional goal. One goal is increased loyalty from existing customers. A second goal is to attract new customers. A third goal is to increase sales clear through the pipeline to end users. A fourth goal might be to make sure pipeline inventories are ready for a seasonal peak such as making sure every repair shop has sufficient AC refrigerant in stock each Spring.
- It is important to distinguish between perishable items with very short shelf life, or items with longer shelf life. It is also important to distinguish whether the items sold are for direct use or for customer inventories.
- The type of promotion can influence sales before, during and after the promotion. A full forecast needs to be done for the entire time span from the time the promotion is announced to customers through the promotion period, and for enough time after the promotion for both customer and distributor inventories to return to normal levels.

Develop a demand forecast:

- Develop a promotional forecast by SKU for every store location that will participate in the program. This forecast should be for sales by time period (monthly or weekly) for the full span of time before, during, and after the promotion.
  - o Sales are typically "normal" in advance of the promotion. However, in cases where the promotion is advertised to end users in advance, there could be some short-term sales decline just ahead of the promotion, as users postpone

purchases until the promotion begins. In theory, those should be made up once the promotion starts.

o Sales should get a good lift during the promotion (or it isn't working).

o Sales might decline for a period after the promotion, as users who "stocked up" at the special pricing work through their own inventory.

- When evaluating the result of the promotion, it is important to include the full-time span of sales versus normal. The results might be overstated if the time periods before and after the promotion are not included.

Develop a plan and detailed calendar for store stock levels:

Inventory managers need to continuously update store stock levels on the promoted SKUs before, during, and after the promotion.

- Increase the store stock level for each promotional SKU on the proper date in advance of the promotion to initiate additional promotion inventory to each store. If the initial inventory is being shipped to the store separately from regular replenishment orders, these data changes need to be synchronized with the arrival of the shipment to avoid triggering unnecessary normal replenishment orders or returns. Maintain that higher order point until the promotion starts.

- Review the sales and inventory results daily. Set a target date and schedule to start reducing store stock levels for each SKU from the promotion level back to the normal level. This wind-down might start about ½ way through the promotion period. This will help avoid shipping additional inventory to the store as the promotion nears its end date. Ideally, the inventory has been sold down to its regular level just as the promotion ends.

- Evaluate remaining on-hand inventory at the end of the promotion. This, too, is a function not available in most supply chain software systems. Ideally, allow any remaining extra inventory above the normal stock level to remain and sell down in the store for some additional period of time, and measure that before triggering any automatic overstock return to the store's distribution center.

Dealing with Vendor offers:

Ideally a vendor will extend promotional pricing and terms for a defined period of time, and allow multiple orders during that period. If that is the case, a distributor can take advantage of it in the following ways:

- An initial order should cover the "pipeline" of extra inventory for stores and some additional inventory for distribution centers.
- Replenishment orders during the promotion should be based on daily sales results and any revised forecasts about how each SKU is doing on the promotion.
- Near the end of the promotion, a "forward buy" order can be placed to take one last advantage of the promotional pricing or terms. The size of this order can be based on actual inventory positions near the end of the promotion, and on the size of the extra discounts or terms. This can provide additional profits after the promotion ends, with purchases at the promotional cost for sales at regular price after the promotion.

If vendors do not allow multiple orders, then a single order must be placed that includes all the forecast incremental sales for the full span of the promotion.

Monitor Daily:

The store stock levels may need to be adjusted several times to properly manage a promotion. Review sales data daily and decide whether to make changes to any store stock levels based on results.

- See Fig. 1 for a suggested promotional management dashboard. Point of sale data and inventory data can be exported daily from most POS systems or data warehouse databases to give the merchant a full view of all affected SKUs and all participating locations during the promotion. This would show sales versus promotional forecast and inventory versus current stock levels. It could allow the merchant to drill down by locations and/or by products to view more detail. For example, in this chart, it appears that the promotion is going nicely in Mid-South states (Arkansas, Louisiana, Oklahoma, Texas), with sales running more than 30% over forecast, and inventories above forecast, too. The merchant might leave those locations as is for now. On the other hand, sales in many of the midwestern states are below forecast and inventories in those states also above forecast levels. The merchant might want to begin to decrease stock levels now in those locations to avoid a big overhang of unsold promotional inventory. In an ideal system, the merchant could make direct changes to Store. SKU stock levels from this dashboard.

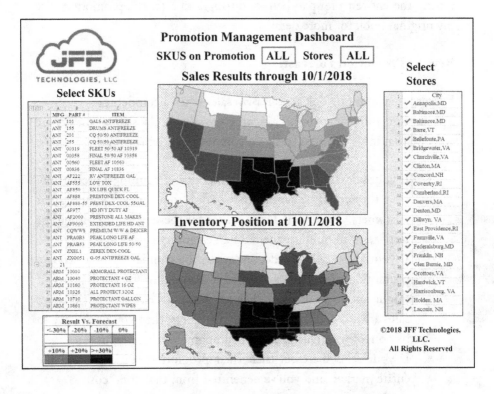

Ch 10. Fig. 1. Promotion Management Dashboard

Evaluate the Promotion at the end of the full cycle:

Evaluate the results once sales levels have returned to normal, likely some period of time after the end of the promotion. Measure overall sales to existing customers to determine if they increased their use or increased their inventory during the promotion. Measure sales to new customers and track their loyalty to see if they continue to purchase, or if they just switched sources temporarily to take advantage of the deal you offered.

Estimating Promotion Profitability:

It is possible to estimate the cost and potential profitability of promotions, by measuring the net change in gross margin at various sales volumes and promotional discounts. Here again, it is important to consider sales during the entire time span before, during and after the promotion. See my original book for more details.

Reverse Promotion Forecasting:

It is also important to look at your own sales when a competitor is running a promotion and you are not. This can give valuable clues about the degree you and that other business really do compete for business on these SKUs.

- If your sales decline while the competitor is running a promotion, then they could be capturing demand from some of your regular customers. They ARE a competitor for these items, and it will be important to monitor them on an ongoing basis.
- If your sales do NOT decline when the competitor is running a promotion, then they are NOT a competitor for these items. It might not be clear where they are getting their sales, but if those sales are not coming from your customers, then you don't have to pay ongoing attention to that company for those items.
- If your sales increase, then their promotion has expanded the entire market, and you've benefitted from that at no cost.

CHAPTER 11

CATEGORY MANAGEMENT

Managing multiple and overlapping product lines can be very difficult for an automotive aftermarket company. Few privately held aftermarket companies have a formal category management function.

For at least the past 30 years, the trend among aftermarket suppliers had been to broaden their offering through mergers and acquisitions of suppliers of related, or in some cases, unrelated other products. As one example, ACDelco offers more than 30 part categories to the aftermarket, ranging from Air Conditioning parts to Wiper Blades. In almost all categories there are multiple quality/price grades, with a wide variety of design, material, or marketing features to differentiate them and justify their price points. Suppliers are good at getting distributors to expand their coverage. "You'll be able to order more frequently if you stock more of our SKUs", or "There is an extra 1% discount if you'll add this additional category or quality grade".

In many categories, the original equipment (OE) supplier also sells OE or OE equivalent parts in the aftermarket. Particularly on high end vehicles, the service shop or vehicle owner is likely to express a preference for replacing an item with the OE brand. These same vendors typically also offer aftermarket parts for many other brand vehicles as well. So, a Mercedes owner can get a set of genuine Bosch spark plugs, but could also get plugs that fit from ACDelco, Champion, Denso, and many other pure aftermarket suppliers. And, a few suppliers offer both their brand name and "private label" generic parts in some of their categories.

There is a full range of distributor owned private label brands, too. Genuine Parts (NAPA) has long led the aftermarket in private label coverage. NAPA Auto Parts likely gets more than 50% of their sales from NAPA branded private label products in the U.S. As one example, NAPA offers 4 grades of NAPA Legend Batteries, Power (economy), Legend (standard), Legend Premium (premium) and Legend AGM (super premium Absorbent Glass Mat). But, even at NAPA, some supplier brands are stocked as well. NAPA Online shows nine SKUs for a set of front disc brake pads for my Ford Expedition – ranging from $34.49 for the NAPA economy grade to $134.99 for Akebono brand premium ceramic pads. Five of those SKUs were in stock at my neighborhood NAPA Auto Parts Store.

Other distributors and program/buying groups began offering private label products about 30 years ago. Only a few old timers remember that the first Bumper to Bumper private label brand name was Rockhill, because Marty Brown, founder of the Bumper to Bumper program group, lived on Rockhill Road in Kansas City. Initially most private labels were in economy grade parts. The CARQUEST group began offering first quality full line CARQUEST brand private labels on major categories in the late 1980's.

Customers, especially professional technicians, often express strong preferences for brands and quality grades they like, and may go out of their normal way to purchase those specific brands. The "decision maker" for the selection of a specific brand/quality grade part for any job varies across shops. In some shops, the technician has the final say, and typically prefers an OE or OE equivalent part whenever that is available, as it is least likely to cause a comeback, and most shops require the technician to perform any warranty work or re-do work without pay. Shop owners typically prefer purchasing from their "first call" supplier as that is likely to maximize the profit to the shop. The technician usually gets more decision making authority on jobs where there is a lot of labor involved. For example, a clutch replacement on a 4-wheel drive pickup truck might be a 4-hour job as it is necessary to disconnect both front and rear drivelines and drop the transmission. A tech really doesn't want to do that job twice.

One of my consulting clients listened carefully to all his customers. If a customer preferred a particular brand or quality grade of an item for some specific make or model vehicles, they would add it to their distribution center inventory. Once customers figured this out, the rate of requests accelerated and the number of new SKUs added to inventory grew rapidly. As a result, this distributor had the most duplicate products I've seen. Here is a chart of the 15 SKUs they stocked in D785 brake pads that fit 1999-2005 Chevrolet Silverado 1500 pickup. Only 3 of the 15 SKUs sold in any reasonable quantity, and 10 of the 15 SKUs sold less than 1 unit per week. But they were all "live" SKUs being replenished when sold.

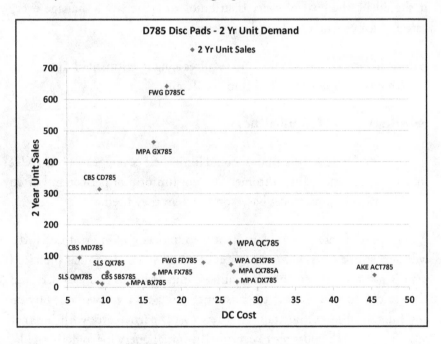

**Ch 11. Fig. 1. Active SKUs for D785
disc pad set at a distributor**

With permission from a consulting client

Category Management:

For many non-automotive companies, category management is a very formal function within the overall merchandising area. The mission is to define the offering in one product category across multiple suppliers, quality levels, price points, and more. Some retailers have internal "category captains". Others enlist a lead vendor to act as category captain, and require that vendor to suggest competing items from other vendors as well as their own items.

There are a number of steps in this process. For more information, see the Wikipedia writeup.[5]

It should be the goal of every distributor to aggressively manage every category for coverage and for data presentation.

It's much harder than it looks, and requires a big investment of time. And, as with lots of topics, the devil is in the details.

Substitution and Cannibalization:

In a "perfect" world, a distributor could limit their coverage to a few SKUs for each application. But customers are not uniform or perfect and often exhibit different preferences based on the item they need.

A huge part of category management is to understand in great detail the willingness of a customer to accept a substitute item when their preferred item is not readily available. It is almost impossible to really understand "lost sales". In many cases, the customer just goes away without buying anything, and leaves no trail. In a few cases, particularly with internet ordering, it may be possible to capture the initial query for something like "Raybestos Brake Pads" and tie that to the sale of a private label item to learn that a substitution worked and the distributor still made the sale.

---

[5] See https://en.wikipedia.org/wiki/Category_management

Cannibalization has also become a serious issue in auto parts category management as many of the value grade items and private labels gained greater acceptance and began to shift sales away from the supplier brand and higher quality items.

Category Management Association:

There is a professional association for category managers, the Category Management Association.[6] It has over 8,000 corporate members and offers a wide range of training programs, member software and data providers, and much more.

A Failed Experiment:

Back in my days at CARQUEST, we tried one extreme experiment. Fuel Pumps were a hotly debated category. Many are in the fuel tank and it is a big job to drain the tank, remove it from the vehicle, clean it, replace the fuel pump, replace and refill the tank. So, technicians usually prefer the OE brand for every application. We assembled a full coverage "CARQUEST NEW FUEL PUMP" private label category by aggregating SKUs from five vendors. We used Bosch as the supplier for all the European makes and models. We used Denso for all Asian makes and models, ACDelco for all GM vehicles, Motorcraft for Fords, and a domestic supplier for all older vehicles and all the other vehicle makes and models.

We assigned part numbers of our own, rather than using the vendor's numbers. That way, we could manage the overall offering to have just one SKU for each application.

We told our customers that they could depend on CARQUEST Fuel Pumps having the very best replacement part for every application – and that they could count on getting a Denso pump in the box for a Toyota, a Motorcraft pump in the box for a Ford, etc.

---

[6] https://www.catman.global/

Unfortunately, it only lasted a couple of years. It required a huge amount of merchant time to make sure we had one product for every application, and to assemble the data for all the catalog vendors to properly present it to customers. None of the vendors were happy with just a portion of the category sales. It took a huge amount of explaining to customers, and many of them still did not trust us to have the best item for each application. We disbanded the effort after a couple of years and went back to multiple lines with lots of overlapping coverage.

ASCM

CHAPTER 12

ASCM

There is a professional association for people interested in or working in the supply chain functions.

The original association in the United States was APICS. APICS began as the American Production and Inventory Control Society. It broadened its scope when it changed its name to the Association for Operations Management. It broadened its scope again, became international, and changed its name to the Association for Supply Chain Management, or ASCM, in 2018.

ASCM has over 45,000 members worldwide.

The bad news is that in all my contacts within the automotive aftermarket, I have met a very small number of people who belonged to APICS or belong to ASCM.

I continue to ask people in the supply chain management in all the automotive aftermarket companies "when you were growing up, was it your goal to be a supply chain manager in an automotive aftermarket company?" No one has ever told me that was their career goal. Almost everyone got to their position in the automotive supply chain with experience in sales or operations, and few have had much formal training in the area.

Virtually everyone, including me, feels they have a great deal of experience with end users and people throughout all the aftermarket. And, virtually everyone feels that experience will enable them to have excellent judgment and make excellent decisions in every facet of their supply chain responsibilities.

But even great experience and judgment should be supplemented with data and "best practices" decision making tools. So, this is an appeal to suggest people involved in the supply chain area of their employer invest the roughly $200 per year to join ASCM. They can take full advantage of a wide range of online and in person training programs and events.

See https://www.ascm.org/ for full details on memberships, training programs, and certifications.

Some years ago I took APICS training programs and I took and passed the test for the CSCP designation – Certified Supply Chain Professional. It was a rigorous training program and a comprehensive exam.

It enhanced my lifetime of experiences with some formal training, and I feel that has improved my ability to help all my consulting clients.

S&OP Process:

It is important for all people and functions within the supply chain and merchandising functions to collaborate and cooperate and implement overall company goals. The best way is a process called Sales & Operations Planning, S&OP. Many companies do not do a good job of this. It is generally performed on a monthly basis. Here is a simplified chart.

SALES & OPERATIONS PLANNING
Working of Sales and Operations Planning Process

Working of Sales and Operations Planning Process

1. **Data Gathering** (Gather data, and prepare statistical forecasts)
2. **Demand Planning Group** (Finalize forecasts, and send them to the Supply Planning Group)
3. **Supply Planning Group** (Ability to meet the demand; If not, what options do we have)
4. **Pre-Exec S&OP** (Prepare a proposal for the Exec-S & OP)
5. **Exec S&OP** (Review, finalize and implement plans)

Ch 12. Fig. 1. Sales & Operations Planning Process Chart

Reprinted with permission from Sketch Bubble.

As you can see, S&OP combines forecasts with demand and supply planning to reach a consensus, integrated solution and get all in the organization "on the same page".

ASCM offers courses in S&OP in most markets, seminars, workshops, and an annual S&OP Conference –scheduled in Chicago, December 3-4, 2020.

ASCM also offers an S&OP Certificate, showing completion of several S&OP training courses.

I urge any reader who is in a supply chain planning, purchasing, or inventory management position to consider joining ASCM.

CPFR – Collaborative Planning, Forecasting and Replenishment:[7]

While it is not directly included in ASCM training, CPFR is an organized way for suppliers, distributors, and retailers to collaborate. It was initially created by Wal-Mart in 1995 and the process was formalized by VICS, the Voluntary Interindustry Commerce Standards Association. The goal is to coordinate forecasts and replenishment between suppliers and customers.

A number of vendors and software providers offer tools to facilitate the data sharing that CPFR requires.

I feel many suppliers and distributors would benefit from this process, but there have been lots of barriers to overcome.

Data security is a big issue. Customers have been reluctant to share their sales data and forecasts with suppliers.

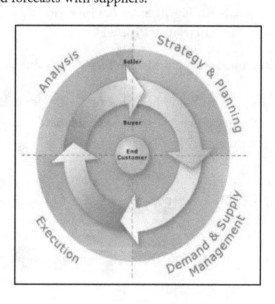

Ch 12. Fig. 2. CPFR Model

Reprinted with permission from 12Manage.

---

[7] https://en.wikipedia.org/wiki/Collaborative_planning,_forecasting,_and_replenishment

I have a consulting client who is an aftermarket supplier and who does not have formal processes in place for S&OP and CPFR, but they should.

They have several levels of forecasts prepared by different departments with only a bit of regular collaboration. They use one forecast for production and sourcing. They support their own brand and several private label brands for major customers. Each of those brands has its own forecasting department to generate requirements for packaging products into each of the private labels and the vendor's own brand. These brand groups do not formally communicate with each other, so if there is a shortage on any SKU, there is no formal attempt to ration it among the various labels.

And, this supplier has access to several major customers' data warehouses, so they have access to complete detail on millions of end user transactions. They could collaborate with major customers to reach a joint forecast and plan for assortment planning and replenishment. When a major customer decided to add emerging SKUs to all its distribution centers and several hundred "hub" stores, it just sent orders to the supplier for that "pipeline" inventory along with its replenishment orders. That really distorted the supplier's forecasting process.

I'm still working on them to update their processes…

OBSERVATIONS ON THE AUTOMOTIVE AFTERMARKET

CHAPTER 13

IMPACT OF COVID-19 ON THE AFTERMARKET

In general, the automotive aftermarket has been much less affected by the pandemic than many other industries. Repair shops, parts stores, distributors and suppliers have all been deemed critical businesses, and the vast majority of locations have remained open in some fashion during the crisis.

The impact on the aftermarket seems closely correlated to the level of Covid-19 cases in most local markets. Distributors in New York City, urban areas in Florida, and similar "metro" initially saw the largest initial decline in sales. A distributor with locations in New York City reported a 75% decline in sales for the first couple of weeks after the lockdown that took effect March 22, 2020. Sales there have come back, but are still significantly below the normal pace. Distributors in other markets have seen much smaller impact. One distributor in a largely rural state reported a 20-25% decline for the first couple of weeks, but a return to within 1-2% of "normal" daily sales in May and June.

The "Before" picture:

The automotive aftermarket has enjoyed a long, steady growth. In general, it is much less susceptible to changes in the overall economy. With data supplied by Harris Williams in May, 2020 and used with their permission, Figure 1 is my view of a strong demographic picture. Total VIO – Vehicles in Operation – in the U.S. has grown steadily from 235 million in 2003 to

278 million in 2019, even with the downturn in new vehicle sales during the Great Recession. The average age of vehicles on the road has increased and is now at a record 12.2 years old. Annual miles driven in the U.S. showed a bit of a dip in the Great Recession, but reached a record level of more than 3.2 Trillion miles in 2019. Vehicles 7 years old and up have grown from 55% to 60% of the total fleet. OE Vehicle dealers have been trying to grow their share of the overall service market for my full lifetime, and have used extended warranties, free service for first several years and other tactics to try to retain the vehicle owner's loyalty. It really hasn't worked and new vehicle dealers still represent only about 25% share of the overall aftermarket revenue from parts and labor services. So, everything looked rosy until Covid-19 emerged.

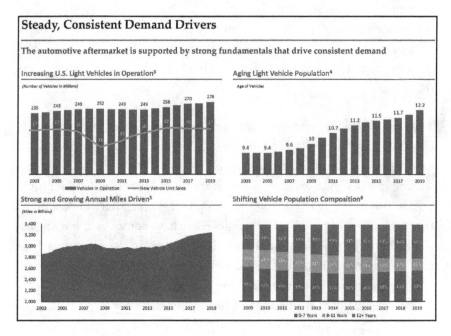

**Ch. 13. Fig. 1. Summary of
Aftermarket Demographics.**

Source data supplied by Harris Williams and used with their permission.

The "During" picture:

Miles driven dropped rapidly as many people did not drive to and from work and followed "stay at home" orders in almost every state. This is starting to recover as states reopen businesses and relax lockdown orders.

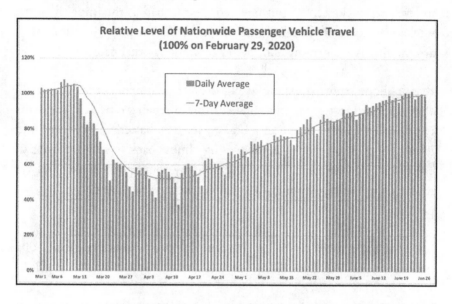

Ch. 13. Fig. 2. Estimate of change in miles driven.

Reprinted with permission from Inrix.

Almost all segments of the aftermarket experienced an immediate, significant drop in revenue as lockdowns began.

It appears the retail "DIY" segment performed better than the professional "DIFM" segment of the aftermarket. AutoZone (NYSE:AZO) reported just a 0.1% sales decrease and a 1.0% comp store sales decrease for its fiscal third quarter – 12 weeks ending May 9, 2020. AutoZone's sales are approximately 80% DIY.

Jefferies held a most interesting 90-minute town hall session with eleven top aftermarket company executives on May 28, 2020. Most indicated a sharp initial drop in revenue in March, 2020, but most said their companies had a much quicker bounce back than they expected. None were back to pre-Covid-19 levels, but all were optimistic for the near term.

So, almost all major retailers, wholesalers, suppliers, vehicle dealers, collision and mechanical repair shops are experiencing a rapid recovery to levels still below 2019, but nowhere near as bad as the initial first few weeks. It is too early to tell if this will hold, but for now, the automotive aftermarket is performing a lot better than many other categories.

Repair shops reported an initial big drop in maintenance work like oil changes. But most reported a smaller drop in repairs, especially for items required for vehicle operation – brakes, starters, batteries, etc. As of mid to late June, some shops were reporting almost back to normal levels of car counts and revenue. This was helped by some pent-up demand for maintenance work, although oil changes were somewhat delayed by the period when the vehicle wasn't driven regularly.

Shops and distributors also reported a big spike in battery sales. Long periods without regular driving (and charging) really damages batteries.

One shop owner said that barring another outbreak, they will make their 2020 goal for a modest increase in revenue over 2019. The bounce back has more than made up for the initial drop.

By the end of July, 2020, a number of public companies began reporting their second quarter results. These continued to confirm the DIY segment is doing the best. Most of the suppliers and most of the distribution companies reported significant revenue declines in Q2 2020 vs. Q2 2019.

For example, Genuine Parts (NAPA) (NYSE:GPC) reported their automotive segment sales decreased 10.1%, and comp sales declined 12.6% in Q2 2020 vs. Q2 2019. GPC has lots of automotive business in Europe and Australia, so this doesn't directly reflect the north American market.

Uni-Select, a Canadian public company (TSE:UNS) reported a 33% sales decrease in Q2 2020. Uni-Select operates automotive aftermarket distribution centers and stores in Canada, and owns Finish Master, with more than 100 locations in the U.S. supplying paint and refinish supplies and equipment to collision shops. With greatly reduced driving and much less traffic congestion, collisions have been significantly reduced.

A very notable exception is O'Reilly Auto Parts (NASDAQ:ORLY). I have long been acquainted with O'Reilly Auto Parts and have a huge amount of respect for them. Their financial report for the second quarter reinforced my respect. O'Reilly reported a 19% sales increase and 16.2% comp store sales increase in Q2 2020 vs. Q2 2019. Their report cited DIY business as the bigger contributor to this increase. Greg Johnson, CEO used the term "incredible" to describe their Q2 operating profit margin of 23.8% of sales. That's the largest operating margin I've ever seen in an aftermarket distribution company. O'Reilly set records for revenue, operating margin and net income in the second quarter. They reported an amazing 50% increase in net income and 57% increase in diluted earnings per share. On their quarterly earnings conference call, they said their business turned up dramatically beginning in the third week in April, when the CARES act stimulus checks and the enhanced unemployment benefit payments began. They said appearance items, performance items, and accessories were the largest growth categories, and felt people not working and with a bit of extra cash worked on their vehicles. O'Reilly was an early adopter of "curbside pickup" and reported growth in online sales. They felt some people might be tackling simpler jobs like oil changes on their own, with some reluctance to visit a repair shop or quick lube and have strangers in their vehicles.

As a result of all this, their stock set an all-time record on the next day. Here is a chart of their stock.

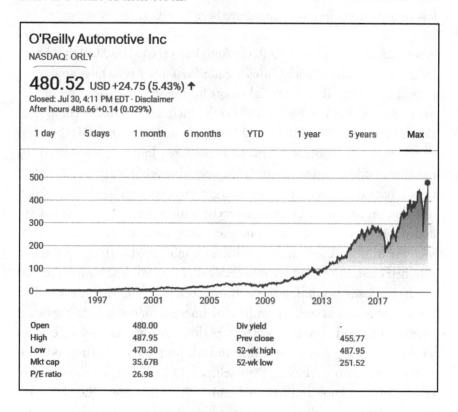

Ch 13. Fig. 3. O'Reilly Stock Chart, July 30, 2020

Google and the Google logo are registered trademarks of Google LLC, used with permission.

Shift to online purchasing:

As evidence of the significant step increase in online purchasing, Amazon (NASDAQ:AMZN) also shattered its prior records with its second quarter, 2020 financial performance. Amazon reported a 40% increase in net sales to $88.9 Billion in the second quarter, and a 100% increase in net income to $5.2 Billion vs. second quarter 2019.

Here is an Amazon stock chart.

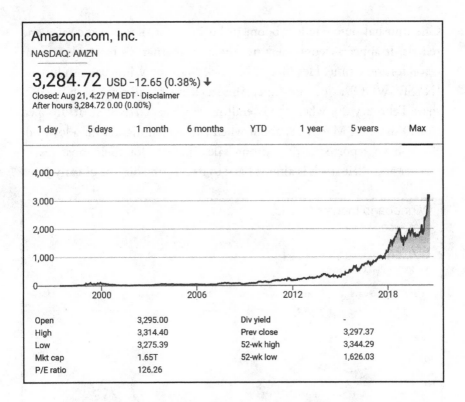

Ch 13. Fig. 4. Amazon Stock Chart, July 31, 2020

Google and the Google logo are registered trademarks
of Google LLC, used with permission.

Coping with Covid-19:

An automotive supplier, Lear Corporation, offered their company's handbook on how to operate a plant safely during this crisis. They have over 250 locations in almost 40 countries worldwide, so they're in areas with a full range of situations brought on by the Covid-19 pandemic. It is an excellent framework for preparing people, policies and facilities. They offer a free download at: https://lear.com/safeworkplaybook. This has a great many principles and practices that are applicable to all kinds of businesses – shops, stores, distribution centers, and many more.

One unusual outcome:

One unusual outcome is a boom in business for motor home sales and rentals. It appears people may use them as alternatives to hotels and air travel for some time. Here is a 2020 stock chart for Winnebago Industries (NYSE: WGO) as of mid-June. The stock hit an all-time high of $62/share February 20, when the overall market peaked as well. It dropped to $20/share on March 18, about when the overall market hit a low. But Winnebago reported a very strong sales increase for their most recent quarter and their stock is almost back to its all-time high as of early June.

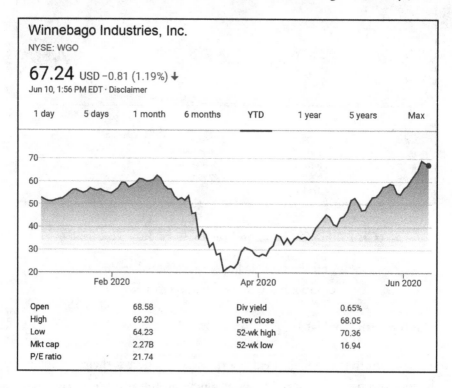

**Ch. 13. Fig. 5. Winnebago Stock
Chart, mid-June, 2020**

Google and the Google logo are registered trademarks
of Google LLC, used with permission.

Miles Driven:

Here is a chart of miles driven with public data downloaded from the Federal Highway Administration through May, 2020. Some are projecting growth from this bottom in the rest of 2020, as it appears many areas are reopening and getting back to a "new normal".

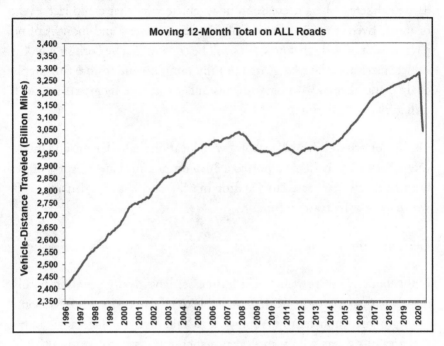

Ch. 13. Fig. 6. Vehicle Miles Driven (billions)

Public Data from Federal Highway Administration Website.[8]

The "After" picture:

It is difficult to predict longer term changes to the aftermarket. It is impossible to predict when miles driven will get back to its long-term fairly steady growth. On one hand, people may take long driving vacations with some apprehension about flying, and people are more likely to drive to work with some ongoing apprehension about all forms of public transportation.

---

[8] https://www.fhwa.dot.gov/policyinformation/travel_monitoring/tvt.cfm

On the other hand, there is likely to be a continued reduction in overall trips away from home for other than work. As much of the aftermarket is dependent on miles driven, this implies it will be impossible to predict when the overall aftermarket will return to its ongoing steady growth of a few percentage points each year.

There is likely to be a decrease in new vehicle sales that could last a year or more. Even with most makes offering zero interest and months of no payments, it is likely that new sales will be constrained by both supply – as vehicle factories take a long time to fully ramp up and restore full supply chains, and demand – as many consumers will face increased financial difficulty for some time.

One major privately held distributor with locations in both rural and metro (New York City) markets reported a 30% drop in revenue in April, 2020, but that decline decreased to 5% drop in May, and was experiencing a 5% year over year increase in June.

Consolidation:

Only about 1/3 of privately held businesses have next generation family members that are ready, willing, and able to take over the business. Some have groomed non family employees to take over management, but a majority of owners who want a reasonably quick way to "cash out" will likely have to find an outside buyer.

Consolidation at Distributor/Retailer level:

The four big, public distributors will continue to get bigger. All entered the pandemic in pretty good financial shape, and all should weather the crisis and return to normal growth quickly as communities reopen fully. And, as the big distributors get bigger, their buying power will continue to increase. This has been obvious as public companies like AutoZone and O'Reilly have a decade long trend of steadily increasing gross margins.

Among privately owned companies, it is very likely consolidation will continue. Most aftermarket distributors were able to stay open during the pandemic, but all had some degree of decline in revenue and income. Many smaller privately held distributors may have significantly impaired balance sheets after the crisis passes. That may even accelerate the ongoing trend of consolidation, and continue the reduction in the number of independently owned distribution companies.

Smaller distributors and smaller buying groups will continue to become less able to compete with the major public aftermarket distributors.

A possible outcome is that some owners may decide to sell or retire a bit earlier than their plan before this crisis, as they might want to avoid any possible return of this pandemic in the future. That implies increased sales among the 2/3 of private businesses that may not have internal management successors in place.

Consolidation at Repair Shop Level:

Aftermarket repair shops have long had a distinct difference in ownership patterns versus many other types of outlets.

In many other categories the norm is for owners to operate multiple locations. Even though this Wall Street Journal article is several years old, I feel it is still accurate.[9] It states that among 60,000 U.S. franchisees of food and restaurants, 36% own multiple locations, and overall, the "big players" own more than 75% of all U.S. locations. This ownership consolidation in non-automotive categories ramped up significantly after the Great Recession, and there is likely to be another round of consolidation after Covid-19.

In the automotive aftermarket, there has been a lot of consolidation in collision repair shops as the significant requirements for becoming a Preferred Provider for the major insurance companies is a complex process and very difficult for single location owners. Private equity has funded three of the "big 4" collision shop consolidators – ABRA Auto Body, Caliber Collision, and ServiceKing Collision. A fourth consolidator,

---

[9] https://www.wsj.com/articles/the-big-get-bigger-1377557950

Boyd Group is a Canadian public company, listed on the Toronto Stock Exchange under symbol BYD.

There has also been consolidation in franchise service chains with the simplest repairs. Tire stores, quick lubes, exhaust and "under car" repair shops all have significant numbers of multiple location owners among their franchisees.

However, there has been little consolidation of full-service general repair shops capable of complete diagnostic and "under hood" repairs of all types. Most shop owners in this category are former technicians. Many have lots of technical experience, and few have extensive business training. So, the norm has been for lots of single location shops in this category. It can be difficult to supervise experienced, very skilled, "A" technicians. They can be pretty temperamental. Many prefer to work for a knowledgeable on-site shop owner, and some may seek a job in another shop if they don't respect the local manager. (The old adage is still true that there is a reason the big mechanic tool boxes have wheels.) So, on one hand, Covid-19 will strain the resources of LOTs of these shops, but there isn't a clear path for owners to sell their shops to consolidators. It will be interesting to see how this plays out over the next several years.

Consolidation at Suppliers:

There has been an interesting split in consolidation activity among suppliers.

On one hand, suppliers who are mostly OE oriented have been spinning off non-core businesses and becoming more specialized. In the past several years Delphi spun off its combustion engine powertrain businesses to focus on electric powertrain and self-driving technologies. Bosch sold its starter and alternator businesses. Continental, a large European supplier, announced plans to split into three companies – Continental Rubber, Powertrain, and Automotive.

On the other hand, suppliers who are generally aftermarket focused have been adding acquisitions to broaden their product coverage areas. One example is BBB Industries, who acquired a turbocharger company to broaden its product line. In general, aftermarket suppliers can offer incentives to customers to buy more or all of their various product lines, and bring more potential customers to each of their categories.

In both cases, private equity has been a major factor in most large transactions.

eCommerce Growth:

In 2020, there has been a step change upward in the ongoing trend of increased on-line ordering for both retail DIY and professional DIFM customers.

AutoZone reported a 50% increase in DIY customer online sales in May, 2020.

Several large service and tire store chains have reported a step change increase in customers making service appointments online.

Cox Automotive, owner Manheim auto auctions and other businesses, switched to an "online only" process for their used car auctions. Prior to this, roughly 50% of used cars were purchased by buyers walking their used car lots.

This may increase the share of on-line resellers like Amazon, Rock Auto, and more. A Wall Street Journal article on May 29, 2020 reported that Amazon will retain as permanent employees 125,000 of the 150,000 temporary workers they hired at the start of the pandemic.

The increase in online business is not just in auto parts. In Q2 Target reported 195% increase, Walmart reported 97% increase, and Home Depot and Lowe's each reported more than 100% increase in online ordering.

IHS Markit Forecasts:

Auto Care Association and the Automotive Aftermarket Supplier Association work with IHS Markit to develop ongoing data and forecasts for the aftermarket. On the next pages are several charts from IHS's forecast as of May 28, 2020. Reprinted with permission. They forecast a big dip, but a very fast recovery and overall continued growth in overall, retail and service channel sales.

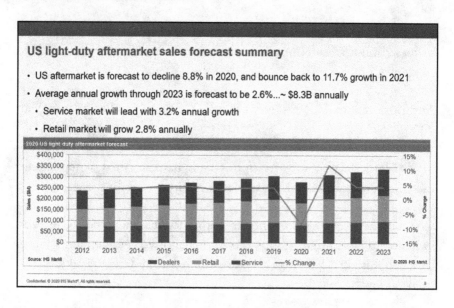

Ch. 13. Fig. 7. IHS Markit U.S. Aftermarket Forecast

Reprinted with permission from Auto Care Association.

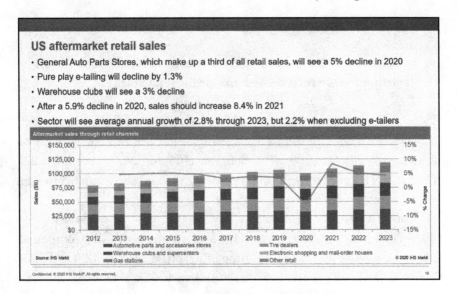

Ch. 13. Fig. 8. IHS Markit U.S.
Aftermarket DIY Sales Forecast

Reprinted with permission from Auto Care Association.

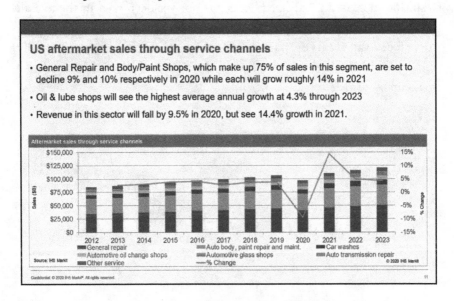

Ch. 13. Fig. 9. IHS Markit U.S.
Aftermarket DIFM Sales Forecast

Reprinted with permission from Auto Care Association.

VIO and VMT Projections:

Projections of vehicles in operation and vehicle miles driven are essential in predicting the aftermarket over the next several years.

Here are some predictions from Derek Kaufman, Managing Partner, Schwartz Advisors, reprinted with permission. The U.S. market exited 2013 with a 248,600,000 VIO. Between 2014 and 2019 there was a 2% CAGR in VIO growth with strong new car sales and decreasing scrap rate.

Schwartz Advisors now forecasts a 16M drop in new car sales during the 2020-2024 period versus the previous 5 years, and a CAGR (Compound Annual Growth Rate) of 1.2%. A drop in scrappage rates in 2020 and 2021 is due to Covid-19 inactivity, but a return to a 4.1% scrap rate for cars and trucks is predicted for 2022 and beyond.

Insurance companies have increased the rate of full write offs of cars due to the increased costs of repairing ADAS and other technologies. The resulting increase in "salvaged" cars has not yet been seen in the overall scrap rates but it is an area to watch. Many foreign markets are now paying more for salvaged cars or "parted out" vehicles than they are worth as fully repaired vehicles. Here are charts with the VIO forecast and current VIO makeup by vehicle type.

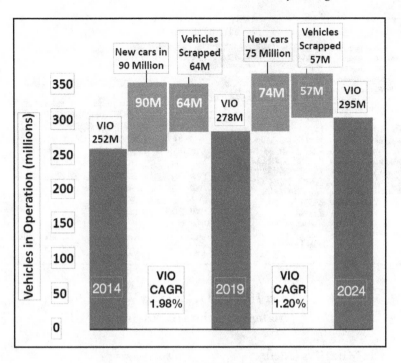

Ch 13. Fig. 10. Vehicles In Operation
Forecast – Schwartz Advisors

Next is a chart of the makeup of the current VIO. Light trucks and SUVs have dominated new vehicle sales for most of the last decade, with those segments accounting for almost ¾ of new vehicle sales in recent years. Their mix in the overall VIO is climbing steadily because of that.

This is good for the aftermarket. An owner of a light truck spends about twice as much on maintenance and repairs as the owner of a mid-size non-luxury passenger car. So, this mix change has caused steady growth in the aftermarket "dollars per vehicle" for parts and service.

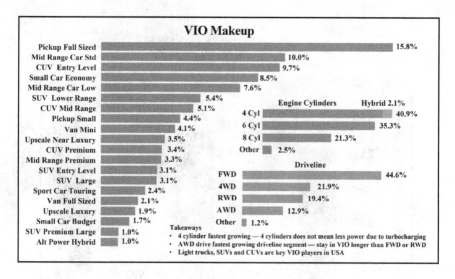

**Ch 13. Fig. 11. Current VIO
Makeup – Schwartz Advisors**

Vehicle Miles Travelled:

Here is a chart with Schwartz Advisor's forecast for Vehicle Miles Travelled. The drop in 2020 from Covid-19 is more severe than the drop during the Great Recession in 2008-09. Commuting represents approximately 30% of total VMT — so the stay at home orders had a huge impact on 2020 VMT.

Schwartz Advisors forecasts the initial comeback will be sharper than the one after the 2008-2009 recession because the underlying economy came into this shutdown in much stronger position than the 2007 economy. It took until 2014 for U.S. to return to 3 trillion miles driven per year.

After the sharp comeback Schwartz forecasts VMT growth matching the rates of 2017-2019 then flattening a bit. Schwartz forecasts it will take 3 years to have VMT cross the 3 Trillion-mile line reaching 3.03 in 2024.

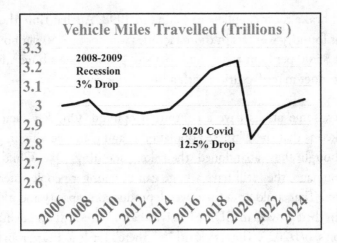

**Ch 13. Fig. 12. Vehicle Miles Travelled –
Schwartz Advisor Forecast**

The China Factor:

Covid-19 and China's actions in 2020 to impose new regulations on Hong Kong both increase strain in the relationship between the U.S. and China.

In 2019 the Trump administration imposed 25% tariffs on many categories of goods, including automotive brake and chassis parts. It is likely those tariffs will continue, and more might be added.

Some in the U.S. have said that the 20th century was the U.S. century and that the 21st century might become the China century. China has had remarkable growth and has reached 2nd place in worldwide GDP.

It has been easy for some to say that the increasing polarization within the U.S., in politics, in income distribution, and in overall opportunity will hamper U.S. growth potential.

Many of those also believe the "managed economy" in China can outperform free capitalism in the U.S. China has targeted and supported manufacturers in a very wide range of products, and their low cost of labor has moved millions of jobs from the U.S. and Europe.

I visited brake rotor suppliers in China in 1998. At that time the hourly wage for foundry workers in those factories was about $.60 per hour. That is about $5.00 per hour today, and that still gives China a huge advantage in all product manufacturing with a high labor content.

However, some others have a contrarian opinion. One key factor often overlooked is that the Chinese population is aging and slowing in growth. Even though they abandoned their long-standing One Child policy some years ago, they still have a huge gap in younger people entering the workforce. That could limit their overall production capacity and ultimately constrain their growth in GDP. Here is a chart from Matthew Klein's article in Barron's, 6/1/2020. The article title is "There's Little to Fear From China's 'Rise'. Why the U.S. Will Probably Prevail in the Long Run". It included this next chart with an estimate of China GDP as % of U.S. GDP.

As you can see, Matthew Klein forecasts China's GDP will peak at 76% of US GDP in 2040, and then decline after that.

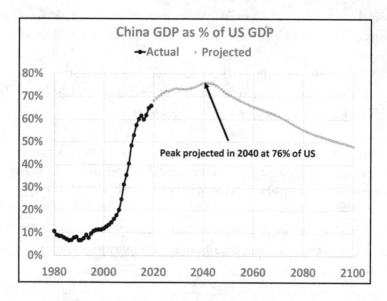

Ch 13. Fig. 13. China GDP as % of U.S. GDP.

Source: Matthew Klein, Barron's, June 1,
2020. Reprinted with permission.

In any case, the Covid-19 pandemic has put huge additional stresses on all segments of the supply chain, and it could further complicate importing auto parts from China.

Many are suggesting North American companies need to rethink their entire supply chain, add flexibility, and add additional sources from other than Asia. Regardless of the source, all supply chain managers will need to be more nimble, flexible, and active than ever before.

Anecdote about Purell:

GOJO was founded just after World War II and for 50 years marketed a special hand soap to mechanics. It was very effective at removing grease and oil, and they built a very nice privately held business around it.

Then, in 1997 GOJO introduced Purell. It took about 10 years to catch on, but the U.S. Army began using it widely in 2005. GOJO's potential customer base went from about 1 million technicians in North America to the entire world population of billions.

I imagine their business took another step change up in recent months.

CHAPTER 14

THE C.A.S.E FOR THE LONGER-TERM FUTURE OF THE AFTERMARKET

Four factors could have major impact on the aftermarket in the longer term. C.A.S.E. has become the acronym for these major items.

"C" for Connected

"A" for Autonomous/ADAS

"S" for Sharing

"E" for Electric

My consulting partners at Schwartz Advisors have done a lot of market research into these four factors and the impact they might have on all levels of the automotive aftermarket. Much of the content of this chapter comes from their work. I apologize in advance for a huge number of new acronyms, but they'll likely become widely used in the aftermarket...

"C" for Connected

V2V (Vehicle to Vehicle) and V2X (Vehicle to Everything) connectivity will impact lots of driving and impact how vehicle owners interface with their vehicle service providers.

Derek Kaufman of Schwartz Advisors makes the point that connectivity changed cell phones into smart phones, and that it will ultimately have the same impact on vehicles. Connectivity can be through cellular or wide area wi-fi network connections. In 2016, Toyota introduced the first vehicles with V2X connectivity, only for sale in Japan. Lots of technology is on the way to improve this. 5G cellular connectivity will greatly expand communication speed.

For driving performance, the Internet of Things (IOT) could eventually make virtually everything a data sender – the traffic lights, stop signs, lane markers, as well as other nearby vehicles, pedestrians, bicycles, and more.

For service, the vehicle's capability to expand data transmission of the full range of vehicle performance parameters, mileage, driving habits, location, and potential service needs could greatly improve the entire vehicle service industry and process.

In the not too distant future, my Lexus might say to me "I'm almost ready for an oil change, and it would be good to get a tire rotation at the same time. Your favorite service provider, Joe's Garage, has an appointment slot at 10 a.m. tomorrow, and the calendar on your phone indicates you're free then. Should I make the appointment?"

"A" for ADAS and Autonomous:

ADAS is the acronym for Advanced Driver Assistance Systems. It encompasses a wide range of vehicle capabilities to help in many driving situations.

ADAS applications will be on 100% of new vehicles in the U.S. by 2025. Some survey data shows ADAS equipped vehicles are about 2% mix of cars in shops now, and that number is growing rapidly.

A major issue is recalibrating the ADAS sensors after a repair. This was first needed in collision shops, but mechanical shops need it too. All cameras and sensors have to be perfectly aligned or they mislead the system.

This will become an issue separating "A" shops – that make the investment in the tools and equipment to perform these new tasks on a wide variety of makes and models, vs. "B" shops will have to outsource the calibration to an "A" shop, or be relegated to simple jobs like exhaust and brake repairs. Even a "simple" job like an oil change requires expertise to know how to reset the dash warning light on some cars. Some BMW models require a special tool to turn off the indicator light.

I rode in a Chrysler in Michigan a few years ago where winter road splash had obscured the adaptive speed control sensor in the front bumper. The car thought there was another vehicle or obstruction right in front of it. It kept applying the brakes, and the car voice kept saying "slow down" … Automatic braking works even when the cruise control is not engaged.

It's an issue in undercar shops, too. You have to do a full calibration of sensors after a wheel alignment, so your car knows it's properly going straight down a road.

Progress in machine learning and artificial intelligence will greatly expand the capability of the vehicle to be aware of everything around it.

Sidebar on ADAS and Automatic Car Washes:

More than 50 years ago I had a great job as the Light Truck Planner in the Product Planning office of the Ford Motor Company. Ford introduced the very first electric door lock option. When the vehicle started moving, the doors locked. It was novel and looked like it would be a big seller. About two days after the new models started selling the phone calls began. They were coming from automatic car washes. You got out of your car and they put it on the conveyor to go through the wash rack. As soon as it started moving, the doors locked. As it reached the end of the conveyor, there it was – engine running, keys in the ignition switch, doors locked, and another car right behind it. It was a big problem. The engineers and product planners had an emergency meeting. The engineers decided 13 miles per hour was faster than any car wash conveyor, so the car doors should not automatically lock until the car reached that speed. They did a panic re-design, recalled hundreds of cars already shipped, and solved the issue. I think Ford is still using that speed, as that is when the doors lock on my fairly new Ford Edge.

50 years later, the automatic car wash companies are going crazy again, as many of the ADAS features are screwing up their life one more time. They're experiencing a whole range of new problems. Here are just a few examples:

- Some vehicles sense they are in Neutral but moving, and automatically shift the transmission into Park.
- In some "push to start" cars, you can leave the engine running, and in neutral gear and hand the car over to the wash attendant. You usually keep the key fob in your pocket. When you get more than about 15 feet away from some of those vehicles, they do some combination of shutting down the engine, shifting the transmission into Park, and/or locking the doors. At the other end of the wash, you're in the waiting area with the fob in your pocket while the attendant can't drive the car off the wash conveyor.
- Some vehicles have "rolling in neutral" sensors that put the car in Park when they sense it is moving with no one in the driver seat.
- Vehicles with automatic wiper systems sometime sense the car wash moisture and turn on the wiper systems. The wipers always lose the fight with the car wash brushes.
- In some vehicles, the adaptive cruise control senses the motion, sees another vehicle just a few feet in front, and applies the brakes.

Up to now, there is no way to turn these systems off, even for a few moments.

So, I had a déjà vu moment a couple of years ago when the International Car Wash Association hired Schwartz Advisors to do a full survey of their 1,500+ members and compile a very specific list by make, model and year – the 2018 Fords do this, the 2019 Toyotas do that, etc. Schwartz Advisors has had the job of compiling the list and helping the association appeal to vehicle manufacturers to solve their specific problems. It's a very long list and most of the vehicle manufacturers just said "thanks for letting us know."

But, in a small victory, the 2020 Mercedes GLS has a Car Wash Button. It does a temporary reset to a bunch of systems to get the car ready for its bath. It raises the suspension (to let the wash clean as much as possible in the wheel wells and under the car), folds the mirrors, makes sure the windows and sunroof are closed, disables the rain sensing wiper system, and lets the car go through the wash in neutral with the engine running. It resets everything to normal operation when it senses the car reaching 12 miles per hour as you drive away after the wash. Maybe car wash conveyors are a bit slower in Europe?

Automated Driver Assistance:

Vehicle manufacturers are counting on Automated driving assistance features to help propel sales of new vehicles for many years to come.

There has been a huge amount of hype and a huge amount of hope that autonomous cars are coming very soon. In my personal case, I hope to buy a fully autonomous car just before someone wants to take the keys away from me.

In 2019, Gartner rated ADAS as having reached the peak of inflated expectations as an emerging technology, even though full emergence is likely more than 10 years away.

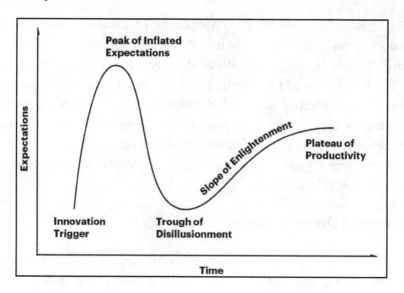

**Ch 14. Fig. 1. Gartner Chart of
Emerging Technologies** [10]

All of the current manufacturers and a number of new entrants are investing very heavily in the technology. A huge new industry is rapidly getting established in sensors, cameras, and very complex computer systems and software to provide autonomous cars. Millions of miles have been logged by Google (now Waymo), Tesla with Autopilot, OTTO (working on trucks and acquired by Uber in 2016), and many other companies.

Even with much more to do, it is very clear self-driving cars have the potential to be much safer than cars driven by ordinary humans. As of this writing, there have been only 5 fatal accidents in self-driving cars, 4 in the U.S. and 1 in China. In one of those, a self-driving UBER killed a pedestrian in Arizona in 2018. No human driver could have avoided that fatal accident, as the pedestrian wheeled their bicycle out into traffic from a gap between a couple of parked cars, and did it right in front of the Uber doing 30 miles per hour. The others were failures of the ADAS systems to recognize an obstruction, or highway lanes, etc. In any case, compare those

---

[10] With Permission. See Gartner Methodologies "Gartner Hype Cycle," 2020. https://www.gartner.com/en/research/methodologies/gartner-hype-cycle

4 U.S. fatalities from 2016 through 2019 with a U.S. average of 35,000+ fatal accidents per year for the past 10 years.

Infrastructure capability is a huge part of this puzzle, too. We need IOT lane markers that can transmit through rain and snow to let the car know exactly where it is under all road conditions. We need IOT traffic signs and signals that can't be obscured by a truck or bus in the next lane. We need completely up to date information on road construction and repair projects and IOT devices in barricades, stop/go signs for one-way traffic, etc. In a perfect world, we need something with a lot bigger range than Bluetooth to sense a phone in the pocket of every nearby pedestrian and bicycle rider. We need V2X to all the cars around us to monitor lane changes, speed changes, and all other driving events. We need full automation of parking garages and parking spaces so you can just tell your car to go find a place to park and wait until you call for it. Your car will also will need the capability to pay any parking fees.

In my opinion, in addition to the technology, this will require a major insurance industry breakthrough. Is the driver really at fault and is the normal insurance coverage in place when an accident occurs and the vehicle is in a full self-driving mode of operation? It really isn't clear today.

Insurance companies are not quick to react, so it might take comprehensive new legislation before self-driving cars can become fully pervasive.

It seems logical that the vehicle manufacturer should bear most of the liability for damages that occur when the vehicle is operating completely in an autonomous driving mode.

As of this writing, Mercedes, Uber, and Volvo have accepted liability responsibility for their vehicles when operated in fully autonomous driving modes.

However, road conditions can have an impact, too, so some highway departments and municipalities could continue to have some shared liability. That may evolve as the need and expectation of "connected" highway and traffic signals, conditions, etc. increases.

Big rig trucks are another story. With well-defined Interstates and generally very good weather in the U.S. southwest, it is almost possible today to create convoys of tractor-trailer trains that could get on the Interstate near the ports of Los Angeles or San Diego and have a huge number of autonomous rigs following the lead of one rig with a driver clear to Texas and beyond. OTTO has done several self-driving tests on I-25 from the Budweiser brewery in Fort Collins, Colorado through the center of Denver and on to Colorado Springs. These were done with full daytime traffic on the highways.

Racing:

Old timers who believe racing improves the breed will look forward to October, 2021. There will be a driverless car race at the Indianapolis Motor Speedway. More than 30 universities have registered. All will receive a standardized race car and will fit it with their sensors and controls for autonomous driving. The race will be only 20 laps (50 miles). The winner has to complete the race in less than 25 minutes. That equates to an average speed of 120 miles per hour. For reference, Simon Pagenaud won the 2019 Indy 500 race from the pole position with an average speed of 175.8 MPH for the 200 laps (500 miles).

Even 50 miles travelled at speed, and the 80 turns in 20 laps will give plenty of opportunities for the participants to test their autonomous driving technology. There isn't much time to react when a car is traveling at about 200 feet per second and is just a few feet away from the next car.

I wish they'd accept entries from Google/Waymo, Uber, Ford, GM, Tesla, as well…

Levels of Driving Autonomy:

The Society of Automotive Engineers (SAE) has established a standard, J3016, with 5 levels of driver assistance.

Level 0 – no automation.

Level 1 – the vehicle includes driver assistance features. Automatic braking is an example of Level 1 technology.

Level 2 – the vehicle has partial automation, but a human driver needs to monitor the situation at all times. Level 2 vehicles may include features like automatic lane centering.

Level 3 – the vehicle has conditional automation. Level 3 vehicles can drive themselves in certain conditions, but a backup driver needs to be ready to take control.

Level 4 – the vehicle has high automation. The vehicle can drive itself without human intervention, but only in areas with the right conditions, or in places that have been fully mapped.

Level 5 – means the vehicle has full automation. Level 5 vehicles can drive themselves anywhere without human intervention.

The Tesla Autopilot is currently rated at Level 2. Audi introduced Level 3 driving in very limited production of its "Traffic Jam Pilot" in the Audi A8 in Europe, but withdrew it in March, 2020.

Hyundai Motor Co., Kia Motors Corp., BMW, and Mercedes-Benz are all expected to have level 3 cars available for consumer purchase in 2021. Prior to Covid-19, it was predicted some Level 4 vehicles might be introduced in 2024. Not sure if that timeline will hold.

So, progress is being made, but lots more needs to be in place.

The full SAE Self Driving Levels chart is on the next page.

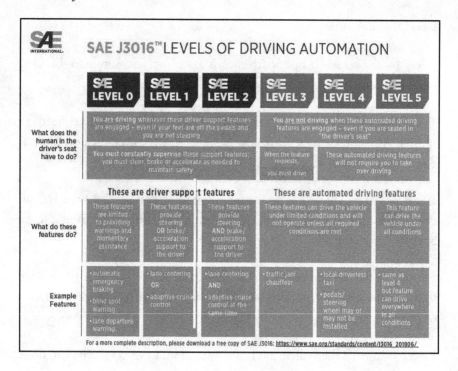

**Ch 14. Fig. 2. SAE J3016 5 Levels
of Driver Assistance**

Reprinted with License from Society of Automotive Engineers

"S" is for Sharing:

The huge expansion of Uber, Lyft and other ride sharing companies has been spectacular. Many people have lived in Manhattan for years without owning a personal car, and that has spread to many other large city metropolitan areas in the past few years.

Before the pandemic, there were about 4 million Uber drivers and about 15 million Uber rides per day, worldwide.

Didi Chuxing or Didi for short is available for use in 400 Chinese cities as well as Brazil, Japan, Australia, Taiwan, Mexico, and Hong Kong. It has 550 million users and 21 million drivers. Before the pandemic, over 30 million rides per day were given by Didi drivers.

So, no wonder that the car manufacturers and many in the aftermarket have been concerned that this could eventually lead to a reduction in overall Vehicles in Operation – VIO in the U.S. and other developed countries.

The pandemic has dramatically changed the outlook. Lockdowns dramatically reduced the total number of driving trips, both in owned and ride share vehicles.

Fear of close contact with strangers may last quite some time, and will be a huge obstacle to people's willingness to use Uber or any of the ride sharing companies. I'm guilty – I have taken exactly one Uber, one regular taxi, and two hired car trips in all of 2020 to date.

A different sharing model with the same potential impact is from Turo and others who provide technology to let a vehicle owner rent their vehicle to others for short trips. On one hand, many people who are likely to be working from home for quite some time will have lots of cars parked in their garages and largely unused. On the other hand, the same fear of close exposure to others is likely to prevent the vast majority of those people from offering their cars for rent to strangers.

Rental car companies are also victims of the pandemic. Hertz Rental Car Company filed for Chapter-11 Bankruptcy on May 23, 2020. In July, Hertz announced it will sell 185,000-200,000 cars, almost half of its fleet.

Opco LLC, the parent company of Advantage Rent A Car also filed for Chapter 11 bankruptcy on May 26, 2020.

Aversion to all forms of public transportation might last some time and increase the use of personal vehicles. So, unfortunately, the pandemic might help the automotive aftermarket in the medium term.

"E" is for Electric / Electrification

Environmentalists have been pushing hard for a conversion to electric vehicles for years. In the U.S., vehicles contribute about 25% of total U.S. emissions according to the "Union of Concerned Scientists". They claim a vehicle emits 24 pounds of carbon dioxide and other gasses per gallon of gasoline consumed. See https://www.ucsusa.org/resources/car-emissions-global-warming.

Almost all electric vehicle proponents cite zero emissions from the vehicle. They generally neglect the emissions from the power plants required to generate the electricity to recharge the car batteries.

In any case, environmentalists have been successful at getting lots of government subsidies for electric vehicles and lots of programs to promote renewable energy generation.

And, in the U.S. and Europe, they've been successful in passing legislation to further restrict emissions from gas and diesel vehicles by tougher emission standards and regulations for ever increasing fuel economy.

- A 2020 European regulation of 95gr/km CO_2 emissions will impose major fines on vehicle manufacturers. This is a 27% reduction from the 2015 regulation at 130gr/km of CO_2 emissions.
- In the U.S. in 2019 under the Trump administration, the EPA issued a new regulation that revoked an earlier regulation that permitted California to set its own vehicle emission standards. The tougher California standards are followed by about a dozen other states. This has been challenged by California and about twenty other states, and the outcome is unknown as of this writing.
- In the U.S. there has been a tax break up to $7,500 for owners who purchase an all-electric vehicle. This tax break phases out over the first 200,000 all-electric vehicles sold by each manufacturer.

    Tesla reached that number in 2019 so no tax break is available to Tesla buyers as of 1/1/2020. General Motors lost the tax break as of 4/1/2020 as well.

However, electric vehicle owners are likely to get a surprise cost of ownership. States depend almost completely on fuel taxes for road and highway maintenance. California, which has roughly 700,000 electric vehicles noticed this first, and passed legislation that takes effect with 2020 model year "plug-in" electric vehicles. These vehicles must pay an initial registration fee of $100 (on top of other fees), and an annual fee of up to $175 to renew their registration and get license plates. That assesses approximately the same fee that gasoline powered vehicle owners pay with the combined federal and state gasoline tax of $.505/gallon in California. The U.S. Federal Government and other states are likely to follow this practice in the future if the mix of all electric vehicles grows sharply.

Even with the tax incentives, all electric vehicles are still much higher in price than gas or diesel vehicles, and they have achieved only a small penetration of the U.S. market. Figure 3 is a chart from Wikipedia, showing cumulative U.S. sales of "plug-in" electric vehicles. This was generated by Mariordo (Mario Roberto Durán Ortiz). He posted it to the Wikipedia article with permission to reproduce it.

As you can see, cumulative sales through September, 2019 are just under 1.4 million vehicles. That is about 1/2% of the approximately 280 million vehicles in operation in the US. During the first nine months of 2019, sales were just over 200,000 units across all makes and models of plug-in vehicles, and that is less than 2% of all vehicles sold in the US during that same period. So, even with lots of incentives, 98% of US vehicle buyers still chose gasoline, diesel, or hybrid makes and models.

Norway has made the most progress, with legislation mandating 100% zero emission new vehicle sales by 2025. I find that a bit curious, since a vast portion of Norway's government incentives for buyers of electric vehicles has come from North Sea oil production.

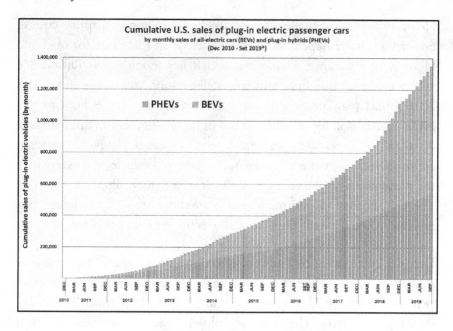

Ch 14. Fig. 3. U.S. Full Electric Vehicle Cumulative Sales[11]

Electric Vehicle Adoption Hurdles

Initial cost, recharging issues, and driving range concerns are contributors to low sales of electric vehicles.

Operating cost savings are supposed to overcome these issues. But, operating costs and overall cost of ownership are difficult issue to assess. One estimated cost of vehicle ownership is at the U.S. Department of Energy Alternative Fuels website, https://afdc.energy.gov/calc/.

Even that does not include the impact of trade-in values, battery replacement costs, and more.

If you live in Oregon with very low energy prices and fairly high gasoline prices, or in California with higher energy prices but much higher gasoline

---

[11] Wikipedia https://en.wikipedia.org/wiki/File:US_PEV_Sales.png

prices, you might break even if you have high annual driving miles, especially in city driving conditions.

In most other places in the U.S., you have to want to own an electric car and accept it costs more.

Recharging is an issue. There are still very few charging stations in most areas of the U.S. "Range anxiety" is watching the battery level decline on a long trip and trying to figure out a charging station location. Recharging time can be an issue, too, especially when traveling. The Tesla Supercharging station takes 20 minutes to reach 50% recharge and about 75 minutes to full recharge.

Replacement battery cost is an issue. Lithium ion batteries do have a definite life. It is generally measured in the overall number of discharge/charge cycles and is typically 500-1,000 cycles. No one tells a Tesla buyer that a replacement battery for their car might be needed after 5 years or so, and might cost $10,000.

Temperature is an issue, too. In January, 2019, Jared Polis, our liberal Colorado governor, signed an executive order to adopt California's Zero Emission Vehicle mandate. This requires vehicle manufacturers to sell an annually increasing percentage of full electric vehicles in Colorado or pay a stiff fine. This executive order, adopted by the Colorado Department of Public Health and the Environment, requires 5% ZEV (Zero Emission Vehicle) sales in Colorado in 2023, with the mix rising after that. As of mid-2019 Colorado had about 25,000 electric vehicles registered, roughly 1/2 of 1% of the almost 5 million registered cars and trucks in Colorado.

Cold weather is an issue that greatly reduces electric vehicle driving range. It reduces the battery performance. The passenger compartment heater, and perhaps seat heaters also reduce the driving range.

In May, 2019, the Society of Automotive Engineers reported on a AAA (American Automobile Association) study of five electric vehicles and their driving range at 20°F and 95°F vs. a baseline at 75°F. They showed reduced cold weather driving range from 50% (BMW i3 electric) to 30% (Nissan Leaf) on these vehicles.

Range reduction would be even greater at Colorado's frequent 0°F winter temps. So, it is unlikely someone could drive any of these vehicles from Denver to Aspen on just one battery charge to go skiing in on a cold day in the winter.

There is also some range reduction at 95°, principally from use of the AC system.

I think most people have some feeling for this reduced range, and that has held back acceptance of many electric vehicles, especially in the northern parts of the U.S.

California, at the other extreme, has a generally mild climate. California also offers a Carpool sticker which lets you drive solo in the HOV lanes with a full electric vehicle, and that can be a huge incentive for longer distance commuters. As a result, 40% of the Teslas sold in the U.S. in 2019 were registered in California.[12]

---

[12] Wall Street Journal 7/2/2020

Figure 4 is the SAE chart on electric vehicle range performance as a function of temperature:

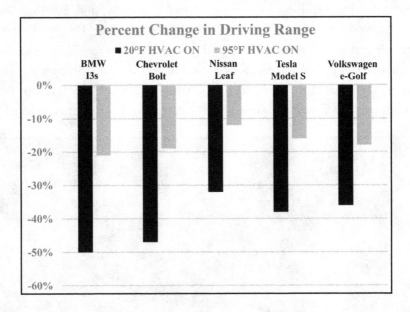

**Ch 14. Fig. 4. SAE Electric Vehicle
Range Changes with temperature**

Reprinted with License from Society of Automotive Engineers

There has been progress from technology and scale in reducing Lithium Ion battery costs. BloombergNEF reports a reduction from $1,100 per kilowatt hour (kWh) in 2010 to $156/kWh in 2019, and projects $100/kWh for 2023.[13] Some experts say $100/kWh is the "tipping point" for electric vehicles to be price competitive with gasoline and diesel powered vehicles.

Electric Commercial Vehicles:

It is an easier story for commercial vehicles, especially city delivery trucks and contractor trucks. These can be recharged overnight to give a full day

---

[13] https://about.bnef.com/blog/battery-pack-prices-fall-as-market-ramps-up-with-market-average-at-156-kwh-in-2019/

of deliveries. One startup company, Rivian, was founded in 2009. Rivian has raised almost $3 Billion in funding, including $700 million from Amazon, $500 million from Ford Motor Company, and $350 million from Cox Automotive. In 2017 Rivian acquired a former Mitsubishi Motor manufacturing plant in Normal, Illinois. In September, 2019, Amazon announced it placed an order for 100,000 Rivian electric delivery vans. The original plan was for prototypes in 2020, production 2021, and completely fulfill this order by 2024. It isn't clear how much that might be delayed.

Ch 14. Fig. 5. Rivian / Amazon Delivery Van

Reprinted with permission from Amazon.

Cox Automotive offers a wide range of services within the automotive channel. They might be considering offering Rivian rental vehicles or servicing through their Pivet division. Pivet currently provides services for almost 10 million fleet vehicles.

Gloomy for the Aftermarket in the very long run:

Some of these C.A.S.E. trends may, in the long run, significantly reduce the total revenue in the automotive aftermarket.

Connected cars will alert owners and service providers when service is needed. The aftermarket really needs to win the legal battle underway now to make sure a car owner can connect his vehicle to any service provider he or she chooses.

Adaptive cruise control and automatic braking are already reducing rear end collisions. I always hope the car right behind me has that feature as everyone seems to be following way too closely at whatever speed I am driving.

As higher levels of driving automation are reached, hopefully collisions will decline even more.

Electric drive may reduce aftermarket revenue, too. The motors appear to be very durable and will likely require much less maintenance and service than internal combustion engines.

Even electric vehicle battery service might not become a big new factor in the aftermarket. When an all-electric car has a massive battery failure, a lot of owners facing a $5-10,000 repair might decide it is time to scrap the car rather than buy an all new battery.

And, the aftermarket is already offering replacement cell packs to allow partial repairs to aging batteries. But, replacing a few cells that have deteriorated is a "band-aid" repair at best.

Sharing is likely to change the aftermarket structure significantly. Vehicle sharing companies will begin to look like huge fleets. They may perform their own maintenance and service at their own large facilities. That could be another big reduction in revenue to individual repair shops and their parts suppliers.

Notes on Tesla:

I confess I'm a bit of a skeptic on Tesla. I acknowledge they have done a great engineering design job, but my days at Ford taught me it takes a whole additional level of production engineering and management to replicate that in millions of almost perfect vehicles.

So, I've missed the whole run up in TSLA stock. I really don't understand that by early July, 2020 TSLA's market capitalization made it the most valuable vehicle manufacturer on the planet.

By August, 2020, Tesla's stock reached another high, and an incredible Price to Earnings ratio of over 1,000. Here's a chart of TSLA stock. Note that this is before TSLA's planned 5:1 stock split scheduled for 8/31/2020.

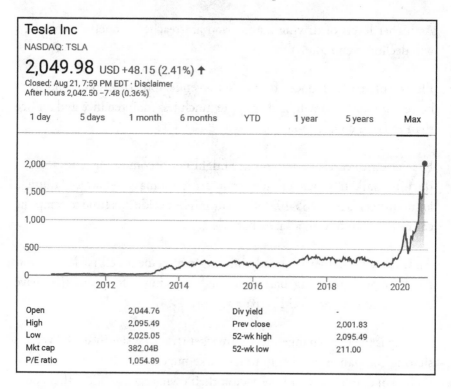

Ch 14. Fig. 6. Tesla Stock Chart

Google and the Google logo are registered trademarks
of Google LLC, used with permission.

It's hard for me to believe a company producing less than half a million vehicles per year, and one that ranked dead last in the most recent JD Power initial quality survey, is worth more than Toyota who produced almost nine million vehicles in 2019.

To a considerable extent, Tesla depends on ways to extract money from governments and entities other than its vehicle buyers.

Tesla's factory in Fremont, California was an abandoned vehicle assembly plant originally operated by NUMMI – New United Motor Manufacturing, Inc. NUMMI was a joint venture by General Motors and Toyota that operated from 1984 to 2010. It assembled Toyota Corollas and several GM models including Chevrolet Nova, Geo Prism, and Pontiac Vibe. Few people knew that these vehicles shared a common "platform". Tesla acquired the site in 2010. It is huge, 370 acres with a 5,500,000 square foot main factory building. It was reported Tesla paid $42 million for the entire site, and it was reported Toyota planned to purchase $50 million in Tesla stock as part of the initial Tesla IPO.[14] So, it was a great deal for Tesla. I do not know how any site pollution issues were handled.

Also starting in 2010, Federal Tax credits of up to $7,500 were available to buyers of zero emission vehicles. This federal tax credit went to the vehicle buyer, and significantly reduced the premium price of a Tesla versus other gasoline or diesel powered vehicles. The tax credits decline to zero as each manufacturer reaches 200,000 zero emission vehicle sales. Tesla reached that level at the end of 2019. So, in total, Tesla buyers received more than $1 Billion in tax credits from the U.S. Government as their rewards for buying Tesla vehicles.

Tesla opened the "Gigafactory" battery facility in Northern Nevada in 2016. Nevada offered incentives including $195 million in transferrable tax credits, 20 years free from sales tax and 10 years free from property tax.[15]

The California ZEV legislation mandates the percentage of Zero Emission Vehicles each manufacturer must sell in California. Only Tesla meets the requirement. All other vehicle manufacturers must pay a large penalty or purchase "emission credits" from companies like Tesla to satisfy their obligation. Tesla's first half of 2020 financial report, filed at the SEC

---

[14] https://www.mercurynews.com/2010/05/27/tesla-paying-42-million-for-fremonts-nummi-plant/

[15] https://en.wikipedia.org/wiki/Giga_Nevada

on 7/28/2020 shows that for the 6-month period ending 6/30/2020 Tesla recognized revenue of $782 million from the sale of "Automotive Regulatory Credits". During that same period, Tesla had an operating income of $610 million, so the vehicle manufacturing business lost $172 million in the first half of 2020.

Tesla is improving. In the first half of 2019, emission credits were $327 million and operating income was a $689 million loss, so in the first half of 2019 Tesla's vehicle manufacturing business posted just over a $1 billion loss.

These incentives are a big part of the Tesla business model. Manufacturing electric cars is a way to earn them.

Tesla has not yet achieved great efficiency at vehicle manufacturing, in spite of huge use of factory robots. At the peak NUUMI assembled about 400,000 vehicles per year with about 5,000 workers. In full year 2019 Tesla produced 367,500 vehicles at this same factory, but had more than 10,000 workers at the plant.

CONCLUSION

CHAPTER 15

CONCLUSION, AND ABOUT THE AUTHOR

I have had a long, full, fulfilling, and rewarding career in the automotive aftermarket.

There have been incredible changes in the almost 70 years since my parents purchased Charlie Hatch's three person machine shop, Hatch Grinding Company. That was in 1951, when I was 7. Here's a picture from the 1940's of Charlie Hatch and his 3 employees. Note the War Bond poster in one window and the '30s panel truck reflection another window.

**Ch 15. Fig. 1. Hatch Grinding Co.,
818 Broadway, Denver, 1940's**

Hatch Grinding Company did about $75,000 sales in 1952, the first full year under the Kornafel family ownership.

My first job, at age 7, for the princely sum of $.25/hour, was cleaning the sludge out of the soluble oil tank on the flywheel grinder.

I got a huge promotion when my second job was to keep the pop cooler filled. I got to keep the money and I didn't have to buy the pop. I saved enough from that to pay cash for a new car when I turned 16.

My third job was learning some of the machining processes. I wasn't strong enough to tighten the collet on the valve refacing machine, but after someone did that for me, I could put a nice new surface on an engine valve.

My father expanded Hatch from a machine shop to an engine parts distributor. He grew it to $1 million revenue. He died suddenly and unexpectedly in his '50's in 1968. My mother ran Hatch by herself for two years.

My wife and I began managing Hatch Grinding in 1970.

We successfully navigated four "all-in", "bet the company" projects, including three major expansions and joining the CARQUEST group in 1979. Each of those transformed our business and took it up to another level.

My wife and I each served a year as Chairman of the Automotive Warehouse Distributors Association, AWDA. We have both been honored with a number of industry awards.

In 1996 Hatch's revenue exceeded $35 million. That's a compound growth rate of a bit over 9% per year for the 45 years it was owned by our family. We had a huge amount of support from an amazing number of fabulous employees, customers, and suppliers.

While I'm proud of that track record, some others have been even more successful. O'Reilly Auto Parts did $700,000 annual revenue in their first store in Springfield, MO in 1958. They've had 60+ years of compound growth over 15% per year and reached $10 Billion in revenue and more than 5,000 stores in 2019.

In addition to our distribution business, I've had the opportunity to participate in a number of other ventures.

I had the pleasure of working with Anders Herlitz when we founded E3 Associates in 1980. We had a great 50/50 partnership. He brought his years of inventory management skills as an IBM software developer. My wife and I contributed the funding and our company as a test bed for new inventory management processes. E3 was a very successful startup and reached profitability in less than 6 months of operation. Anders gave us more than a venture capital return on our investment when he bought us out after the first couple of years. He went on to build E3 into a good size company. He sold E3 to JDA in 2001 for $50 million, and E3's technology is still at the heart of JDA's supply chain software offering. This was one of the very few times in my life when I had even a tiny bit of remorse (that I didn't keep a small percentage of ownership). But the automotive aftermarket has been very rewarding to the Kornafel family, so I quickly got over that and went back to work.

We merged Hatch Grinding into General Parts, Inc. in 1996, and I had the opportunity to serve as President and then Vice Chairman of CARQUEST Corporation until 2013.

In 2014 I formed JFF Technologies, LLC to offer my services as an inventory consultant to aftermarket companies. I have learned lots from every engagement and client.

In 2015, Rick and Mort Schwartz expanded Schwartz Advisors into a full-fledged aftermarket consulting company with the addition of a number of professionals. It has been an honor to be a Partner of Schwartz Advisors, and I've learned lots from their many clients.

When there were just a few makes and models of cars and they didn't change often, life was a lot simpler. The Fram PH8A oil filter was used on some Ford cars from 1957 through 2003. Today, there are more than 1,000 make/model/engine combinations for every model year. I've watched the industry grow from a few thousand to many millions of SKUs.

So, for all of my career, and for the foreseeable future, inventory management is a necessary survival skill. I hope you will benefit from some of the ideas in this book.

APPENDIX 1

ABOUT SCHWARTZ ADVISORS

Mort Schwartz has a full career in the automotive aftermarket, at suppliers, distributors, and as a consultant. One of his sons, Rick Schwartz has been an automotive aftermarket consultant for almost 15 years.

In 2014 a number of other aftermarket veterans, including me, joined Schwartz Advisors as Managing Partners, Partners, and participating consultants.

Schwartz Advisors offers buy side advisory services, principally to venture capital firms considering investments in the aftermarket, sell side advisory services to a wide range of automotive companies who are planning to sell or seek investor partners, and strategic consulting services, also to a full range of automotive aftermarket companies.

The current group of eleven has very broad experience. An attorney and a CPA financial expert offer negotiation, valuation and structure opinions to both buyer and seller clients. One Managing Partner has wide experience in the heavy-duty segment. Four have wide experience at automotive component suppliers. Another is also Executive Director of the University of the Aftermarket, in conjunction with Northwood University. I bring my experience in the distribution and inventory management areas.

Schwartz Advisors currently has more than ten projects in process across all three practice areas. The aftermarket business goes on, even in the midst of the Covid-19 pandemic.

I wish to acknowledge and thank Schwartz Advisors for some of the content of this book, particularly in the chapters with observations about the aftermarket.

Please see www.SchwartzAdvisors.com. The site includes a wide variety of "Insight" white papers in addition to information about all of Schwartz Advisors services.

APPENDIX 2

WWW.INVENTORYCHAMP.COM

In my work with automotive aftermarket companies and distributors, I have learned that many supply chain software packages lack some "best practice" features for several special situations.

So, I designed www.InventoryCHAMP.com to include three online calculators for these situations:

1. An Economic Order Quantity – EOQ – calculator that includes the ability to evaluate a SKU level quantity discount or cost savings.

2. A Forward Buying calculator – to evaluate the profit and return on investment opportunity for "one time" offers from a supplier. The model can evaluate the impact of an extra discount, extended payment terms, an imminent cost increase, or a combination of any or all of those temporary deals.

3. A SKU Safety Stock calculator. This includes some "real world" corrections vs. the pure statistical math used in most other systems.

A paid subscription is required to use the online calculators. You can subscribe for 1 day, 1 month, or 1 year.

Each of the calculators has an example. Subscribers can input their own parameters and get the results in graphic form like the examples below.

Subscribers can save their models and recall them for future similar situations.

EOQ:

The classic EOQ model does not provide for situations where a quantity discount or other savings are possible. The InventoryCHAMP model has been enhanced to include that. If your firm can earn a discount or have other savings by ordering in a specific amount, enter the amount required to achieve the discount and either the discounted item cost or discount percent. In some cases, this might be a discount provided by a vendor for ordering a specific amount. You should also examine your own costs for potential savings. In our auto parts distribution company, it was more efficient to receive the most popular SKUs in full pallets. Even though there was no purchase price reduction, our shipment receiving costs were lower if we placed a full pallet of one SKU into a pallet picking location versus stocking multiple units onto a shelf by hand. A popular air filter or brake rotor might have 100 units on a pallet. We felt we saved about $5 in receiving cost when we received a full pallet of one SKU. That effectively reduced our cost by $.05 per unit. The Sample Project is an analysis of this situation, and it shows even this modest savings is enough to suggest purchasing the sample SKU in pallet quantities.

Example: A SKU has annual forecast demand of 1,200 units. It costs $25.00. Assume 25% inventory carrying cost rate and $10.00 to handle a receipt. Assume the vendor offers this item in pallets of 100 units.

The receiving cost savings of $5.00 = $.05/unit. Even this modest savings is enough to suggest it is better to purchase this SKU in pallet quantities.

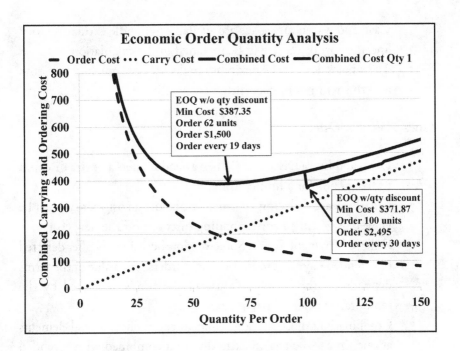

Appendix 2. Fig. 1. EOQ with Quantity Discount

Forward Buying:

Forward Buying is an opportunity to place a larger than usual order when a vendor offers some temporary or one-time incentives. This can be a source of additional profit. ALL of these conditions must be true for a purchase to qualify as a Forward Buy:

- This offer is not likely to be repeated soon.
- The merchant does not pass the special terms on to customers. (If the terms are passed on to customers, this is a Promotion, not a Forward Buy.)
- For cost increases, the merchant will implement a matching selling price increase concurrently with the cost increase, so that the amount of the selling price increase is captured as additional margin on goods purchased before the cost increase goes into effect.

- Cash and warehouse space are available to handle extra inventory, and the cost of those will be included in the calculations.
- The wholesaler has the flexibility to decide how much to buy now, and this will not impact future availability.

Types of Vendor Offers:

- Deals and Extra Discounts: When a vendor offers an extra discount or free goods for a limited time.
- Cost Increases: Placing an order just before a cost increase can be viewed as getting a corresponding discount off the new cost.
- Deferred Payment Terms: Some vendors occasionally offer deferred or extended payment terms on single orders. The value of the terms depends on the merchant's use of the funds generated by the temporarily deferred payments.
- Combinations of Deals: Sometimes a vendor offers several elements at one time – such as an extra discount combined with extended terms. These combinations can be very valuable Forward Buying opportunities.

Forward Buying Example:

You have an opportunity to place an order just before a 4% cost increase goes into effect. You normally order $1,000 per week in this category, and you are ready to place your regular weekly order. Assume an inventory carrying cost of 25% per year, a 5% cost of funds, and a $5 cost to receive a shipment. Also assume you raise your selling prices at the same time the vendor raises your cost, so your company will make the extra margin on all units purchased above the regular quantity.

Here is a chart of extra profit and ROI on extra investment for varied order sizes.

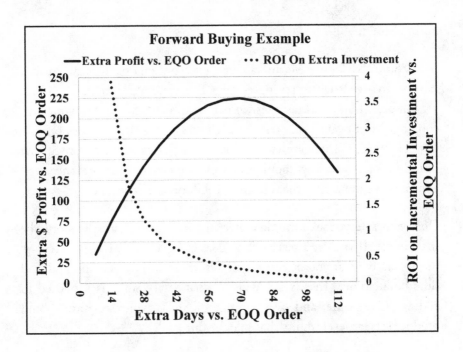

Appendix 2. Fig. 2. Forward Buying Example

The maximum incremental profit of $225 would occur with a 70-day order. That is 10 week's supply or a $10,000 order. That gives about a 30% return on the average incremental investment of $4,500 (1/2 the extra order amount) over the 70 days it will take to use up this large order. In the real world, it is typical to place an order for about 2/3 of the optimum amount. That hedges for some forecast inaccuracy and other considerations such as balancing the next orders, and the potential for another deal.

Users are cautioned to not mix Forward Buying with Promotions. If your firm passes through any of the extra offer, it is really a promotion, not just a forward buy. That requires a different analysis. In some cases, it is possible to use promotion forecasting during the promotion, and then do one forward buy just at the end of the vendor's special offer.

Safety Stock:

Safety Stock is a lot like Marinara sauce. Everyone guards their own recipe. No one divulges their secret ingredients. Everyone seems to like their own version best. In a blind taste test, it can be difficult to identify your own cooking. Most evaluations are qualitative, not quantitative. But, on that last comment... There are two simple quality tests for safety stock that would be very revealing about your software's overall performance. Yet, almost no vendors offer them in their ERP software packages.

Does your safety stock formula deliver the requested results? It should be that simple. If you set a service level goal of 98% on a SKU or category, that's exactly what you ought to get. Yes, there will be demand and lead time fluctuations. That is EXACTLY what safety stock is supposed to address. Over time, and over a range of SKUs, your software should produce service level results that match your goal.

Do you have the expected amount of safety stock inventory? Your "on hand" inventory just before you receive a shipment is the actual safety stock. It should be easy to compare that actual inventory to the computed, desired safety stock to validate your software's performance.

These two measures would validate that your safety stock formula delivers the service levels you desire, and that you have the expected amount of safety stock inventory investment. If your software system offers these two measurements, use them!

Many inventory software packages use a "classic" safety stock computation, based on the Normal Distribution. The Normal Distribution accurately predicts the probability of random, independent events. For example, it will accurately predict the probability of a specific number of "heads" in tosses of a "fair" coin.

Some software packages use a safety stock formula that sets safety stock to achieve a percentage of stockouts, not a service level. A formula that predicts a SKU will not have a stockout in 98% of replenishment cycles is NOT the same as asking for an overall 98% order fill service level.

In our auto parts distribution business, the "real world" does not exactly follow the pure Normal Distribution statistics. Not all demand "events" are truly independent and random. Brake rotors are mostly sold in pairs, so demand events are not "independent". If an item has a relatively high rate of alleged warranty claims, we encounter an additional demand for a SKU shortly after some sales as a warranty replacement. That is not random. Events often bunch up. When the market is "hot", demand is above forecast, and our vendors may take a bit longer than usual to process the larger orders. So, high demand variability and longer lead times are often in sync, and not independent.

The InventoryCHAMP.com formula has an empirical correction to the pure statistics. That is JFF's "secret ingredient". It is based on many observations to tweak the statistical tables until users achieved the goal they set on "real world" SKUs. JFF typically requires more safety stock than most other package results.

The JFF model can be a good way to compare safety stock results to your own software package to help you achieve your desired results. Here is a chart of JFF's safety stock vs. the classic Normal Distribution model for a typical SKU.

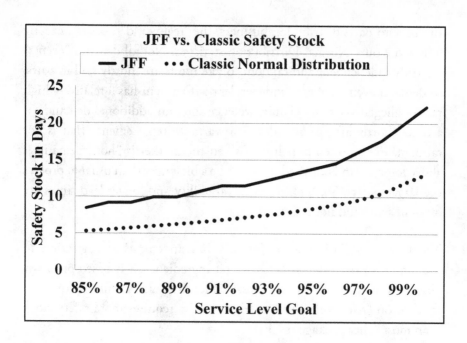

**Appendix 2. Fig. 3. JFF Safety Stock
vs. Normal Distribution Models**

I hope you'll browse www.InventoryCHAMP.com and let me know if you have comments, criticisms, or suggestions.

Please contact me at pete@petekornafel.com with any and all feedback.

INDEX

W

Waymo 146
When gone use 95
Winnebago 126
work order data 14
WORLDPAC 32, 77, 93

Y

YMME 5, 6, 11, 16
Your Car, Your Data 22

Z

Zero Emission Vehicle 155
ZEV 155, 161

CPSIA information can be obtained
at www.ICGtesting.com
Printed in the USA
BVHW031827221020
591574BV00005B/40